STUDIES ON INDUSTRIAL PRODUCTIVITY:
SELECTED WORKS

Volume 8

A DIFFERENT TRANSITION PATH

A DIFFERENT TRANSITION PATH

Ownership, Performance, and Influence of Chinese Rural Industrial Enterprises

CHENGGANG XU

Routledge
Taylor & Francis Group

LONDON AND NEW YORK

First published in 1995 by Garland Publishing Inc.

This edition first published in 2019
by Routledge
2 Park Square, Milton Park, Abingdon, Oxon OX14 4RN

and by Routledge
711 Third Avenue, New York, NY 10017

Routledge is an imprint of the Taylor & Francis Group, an informa business

British Library Cataloguing in Publication Data
A catalogue record for this book is available from the British Library

ISBN: 978-1-138-61548-9 (Set)
ISBN: 978-0-429-44077-9 (Set) (ebk)
ISBN: 978-1-138-31430-6 (Volume 8) (hbk)
ISBN: 978-0-429-45706-7 (Volume 8) (ebk)

Publisher's Note
The publisher has gone to great lengths to ensure the quality of this reprint but points out that some imperfections in the original copies may be apparent.

Disclaimer
The publisher has made every effort to trace copyright holders and would welcome correspondence from those they have been unable to trace.

A DIFFERENT TRANSITION PATH

OWNERSHIP, PERFORMANCE, AND INFLUENCE OF
CHINESE RURAL INDUSTRIAL ENTERPRISES

CHENGGANG XU

GARLAND PUBLISHING, INC.
NEW YORK & LONDON / 1995

Library of Congress Cataloging-in-Publication Data

Xu, Chenggang.
  A different transition path : ownership, performance, and influence
of Chinese rural industrial enterprises / Chenggang Xu.
      p.   cm. — (Garland studies on industrial productivity)
  Includes bibliographical references and index.
  ISBN 0-8153-1629-1 (alk. paper)
  1. Rural industries—China.   2. Right of property—China.
3. Privatization—China.   4. Rural development—China.   I. Title.
II. Series.
HC427.92.X83   1995
338.951—dc20   94-46983
                                                                CIP

To my parents

CONTENTS

PREFACE

Two chapters in this volume are based on my Ph.D dissertation; thus my first acknowledgements should go to my dissertation advisers: Professors Janos Kornai, Eric Maskin, Andreu Mas-Colell, and Dwight Perkins. I must admit that I would not have reached my current ideas about socialist economies and socialist reforms without having been exposed to Janos Kornai's penetrating thinking. As a scientist from a ruthless society who is concerned about truth, freedom, and justice, Professor Kornai not only has taught me academically, but also has greatly inspired me. I owe a great debt to my teacher and supervisor Eric Maskin who has trained me in economic theory. He is the most rigorous and altruistic teacher I have ever met in my life. His deep understanding of economics and his endless curiosity, together with his sharp and provocative criticisms, have greatly affected my way of thinking. I am also deeply indebted to Andreu Mas-Colell, whose profound and elegant thinking has enlightened me. His broad interests, generosity, tolerance, and very natural sense of humor have always provided me with great encouragement, especially in times of trouble. I am extremely grateful to Dwight Perkins. His thorough understanding of the institutions of developing economies, and of the Chinese economy in particular, has guided me not only in my dissertation, but in my research in general. I still draw enormous benefit from his insights. Moreover, he has helped me in many personal and critical ways from the very beginning of my studies at Harvard. I shall always be indebted to him.

I should thank Martin Weitzman in a special way. He was very generous with his advice and encouragement, particularly on my research related to TVEs and Chinese economic reforms when I was a student. But his influence on me, through our conversations and my reading of his works, goes far beyond these topics. I have greatly benefitted from his theories on economic systems, centrally planned economies, and economic organization in general. I feel fortunate to have had the opportunity to work with Marty and I continue to learn from him.

My research on Chinese township-village enterprises (TVEs) began in the summer of 1985 when I worked at the World Bank with William Byrd and wrote the first background paper for the World Bank-Chinese Academy of Social Sciences joint research project on TVEs. Since then I have written several papers on related topics. This volume is a collection of some of my work on the topic. Chapters one and three are from my unpublished dissertation, and chapter two is a reprint of a paper, which is published in *Journal of Comparative Economics*, co-authored with Martin Weitzman.

For their comments on all or part of the work collected in this volume, I like to thank C. Bai, J. Berliner, S. Fischer, R. Gordon, J. Green, O. Hart, A. Hussain, D. Jorgenson, D. Li, M. Lu, J. Moore, L. Putterman, Y. Qian, G. Roland, A. Sen, T. Sicular, and N. Stern.

I am grateful for financial support to the Harvard-Yenching Institute Doctoral Scholarship, to the Suntory-Toyota International Center for Economics and Related Disciplines (STICERD), and to the Center for Economic Performance (CEP) at the London School of Economics. Moreover, I thank the hospitality of the Harvard Institute for International Development which has supported my work in the preparation of this volume for publication.

Special thanks go to Nancy Hearst. As a knowledgeable librarian, she has drawn my attention to many important sources which I otherwise would not have noticed and has spent countless hours of time editing my writing.

I am deeply grateful to my wife Kuanghui. She has been a sympathetic and critical listener. Her love, understanding, encouragement, and advice have always been essential at all stages and in all dimensions of my struggles.

Cambridge, Massachusetts   Chenggang Xu
September 1994

A Different
Transition Path

Chapter 1

Introduction

In recent years, it has come to be widely recognized that the township-village enterprise (TVE) has been the most important engine driving the unprecedented growth of the Chinese economy during the last 15 years; and the development of the TVE is the most important feature which distinguishes the Chinese transition path from those of the former Soviet Union and Central-East Europe. A TVE is a collectively-owned communal enterprise located in a township or a village. All the residents of the township or village that has established the TVE own the firm; the property rights of the TVE can only be executed collectively through representatives of the community. Thus, there is deep involvement of the community government in the TVE's operations. Regardless, the TVE in fact has been enormously successful. Its growth performance is outstanding by world historical standards. And the TVE growth rate largely accounts for the difference between the growth rate of the aggregate national industrial output and the growth rate of state-owned industries.

The spectacular growth of the TVE sector raises important questions: Apart from its growth rate, how efficient is the TVE sector compared with the state sector? What are the regional differences in TVE efficiency? What are the sources of such efficiency? The first chapter of this volume will address these questions. It first analyzes the institutional background of the TVE, and then will try to answer these questions by analyzing provincial-level panel data (1982-1987). This chapter was written four years ago. Although the data could be updated,

I believe most of the findings drawn at that time are still valid.

The econometric analysis in this chapter shows that the TVE sector is much more efficient than the state sector: the growth rate of the total factor productivity (TFP) and the share of TFP growth in the growth of the TVE output are many times higher than those of state-owned enterprises (SOE). Moreover, in terms of the high TFP growth rate and high share of TFP growth in the growth of output, the Chinese TVE sector displays some similar features to the Japanese economy in the 1960s and to the South Korea economy in the 1970s. With respect to the regional differences in efficiency, I find that TVEs in large metropolitan regions are in the best position to get better technologies, but are probably in the worst position in terms of being controlled or influenced by the bureaucracy. In contrast, TVEs in coastal regions probably are in the best position to avoid bureaucratic controls. Comparing the level of the TFP and the growth rate of the TFP in TVEs in different regions, TVEs in large metropolitan regions have the highest initial TFP level and the lowest TFP growth rate, while TVEs in coastal regions have a moderate initial TFP level but the highest TFP growth rate. In interior regions, the initial TFP level is the lowest, but the TFP growth rate is higher than that of those in large metropolitan regions.

With respect to employment behavior of TVEs, based on pre-1988 data, I find that statistically the wages of TVE employees have little to do with competitive labor markets; instead, they are similar to the wages of the nearby state-owned enterprises and urban collectively-owned enterprises. This indicates government control over TVE wages. Moreover, TVE workers' income is significantly lower than the marginal product of labor (this is reconfirmed by a later study by Pitt and Putterman, using firm-level panel data, 1993). This finding is consistent with some reported casual observations that underemployment exists in some of the areas where TVEs are concentrated, although a labor surplus is a general phenomenon in most Chinese rural areas. This indicates the possibility of inadequate migration.

The high efficiency outcome and the seemingly inefficient allocation of labor input of TVEs is enigmatic. If we take a closer look at the TVE institutions, such as property rights, then we find that the typical TVE is quite different from a well-defined private firm. According to standard property rights theory, the existence of well-defined private property rights should be an essential precondition to the proper functioning of a capitalist market economy. My second chapter focuses on the paradoxical success, despite the lack of well-defined private property rights of the Chinese township-village enterprises. This chapter argues that a TVE is best described as a vaguely-defined cooperative, essentially a communal organization without a well-defined ownership structure. The extraordinary success of the TVEs presents a severe challenge for traditional property rights theory: Why do vaguely-defined cooperatives perform so well? Is this not in contradiction with the basic precepts of property rights theory?

To answer these questions, in chapter two we argue that standard property rights theory assumes that all people are indiscriminately non-cooperative. Under this assumption, a major role of ownership is to resolve conflicts or to enforce cooperation in an economic organization. However, if there are other mechanisms which are different from formal contracts and/or property rights, or if there are variations in cooperative behavior among people of different societies, then the significance of ownership to solve conflicts in economic organizations may also vary.

By using a fundamental concept of repeated game theory, we try to integrate formally other noncontractual mechanisms, or the seemingly cultural element of a cooperative spirit, with standard property rights theory to arrive at a more general version of property rights theory. The general approach proposed in this chapter may reconcile the originally-posed paradox.

This chapter was written two years ago and is reprinted from the *Journal of Comparative Economics*. In the two years since the circulation of this chapter, I have come to realize that the theory proposed here can be applied to explain more phenomena than we originally expected. In addition to vaguely-defined cooperatives such as TVEs, it also sheds light on informal financial institutions, informal relationships, and implicit contracts in inter-firm transactions and in internal organization. These informal financial institutions and informal relationships within and between organizations are very popular and play essential roles as partial substitutions for formal rules, contracts, and ownerships, particularly when market imperfections are severe. Because the development of market system and well-defined property rights is both complex and complementary, the lack of proper conditions to develop substitute mechanisms may result in different economic development path. As a matter of fact, there were a lot of informal relationships, and informal institutions, which greatly helped the development of the economies of Taiwan, South Korea, Japan, and of China during the period between the late nineteenth century and the 1950s.

Finally, I believe that this theory is more relevant to village enterprises and to those township enterprises which are related to the local township residents. In such cases people live together and know each other well, and their relationships are repeated over decades or generations.

The third chapter deals with some rural-rural and rural-urban migration phenomena which have accompanied the development of TVEs and which cannot be explained by existing theories. The finding in the first chapter that the marginal labor productivity is lower than the wage in the TVE sector is confirmed by the observation from sample surveys that people in poor rural areas migrate more to rich rural areas, where wages are higher than in the poor rural areas but lower than in urban areas, than migrate to urban areas; in contrast rich rural area people migrate to urban areas. This raises some puzzling questions: why do people in poor rural areas, where surplus laborers result in a serious low marginal labor productivity, migrate less to urban areas than people in rich rural areas? Why do so many people in poor rural areas migrate to rich rural areas where wages are lower than urban wages, while many rich rural area people migrate to urban areas?

The third chapter provides a theory to explain these phenomena. The theory is based on the nature of the risks faced by out-migrants and their families -- regarding rural households as geographically extended cooperative families.

Facing the high risk of price fluctuations to meet basic needs, such as housing and food (in this chapter we use food prices as an example), a geographically extended cooperative household which has land and has out-migrants regards city jobs as high-risk high-income opportunities, and regards agricultural production on its own land as low-risk low-income opportunities. Because agricultural outputs from their land are not affected by price fluctuations, agricultural production serves as an insurance for rural households: in a bad year with high prices, the household can survive by relying on their own agricultural output. In order to insure themselves, risk-averse rural households keep more labor input in agriculture (i.e. reduce the number of rural-urban migrants) compared with risk neutral households. Therefore, the "excess" labor input in agriculture, and the resulting lower marginal labor productivity in agricultural production, becomes the virtual payment for the insurance of rural households.

Regarding migration as an instrument of the income portfolio of a household, in an economy where most rural households have land, if poor households are more risk averse than rich households, then with respect to insurance, a poor rural household will have fewer rural-urban migrants than a rich rural household. With safer real incomes in agricultural jobs, many members of households in poor rural areas migrate to rich rural areas, up to the point that the marginal labor productivity in the poor areas equals that in the rich areas. An important implication of this result is that the gap between the rich and the poor is widened when there are opportunities for rural laborers to migrate to cities, and when migration provides more opportunities to earn higher incomes. Three years after this chapter was written, we observe this unfortunate phenomenon clearly.

The theory in this chapter may provide some clues to explain the differences between the reformed Chinese economy and some other developing economies: in China, almost all of the rural households have land, rural-urban migrants face big uncertainties in the markets, and a limited rural-urban migration is observed; in other developing countries, a notable number of rural households are landless, rural-urban migrants are not as clearly differentiated from regular urban residents in the markets as they are in China, and migration-related unemployment is a distinguishing feature. When the uncertainty in the markets is reduced, and migrants are less differentiated from regular urban residents, urban-rural migration may increase. In fact, this is exactly what has recently occurred in China recently--three years after this chapter was written.

Chapter 2

Productivity and Behavior of Chinese Rural Industrial Enterprises

INTRODUCTION

One of the most spectacular changes in China's economic reforms from 1978 to 1988 has been the rapid growth of rural industry which is a nonstate industrial sector. The study of the growth and behavior of Chinese rural industry will not only benefit our understanding of the Chinese economy, but will also broaden our insights on socialist reforms and on economic development.

There is a small but growing body of literature on Chinese rural industry. Perkins and Yusuf (1984), Riskin and Sigurdson (1977), American Rural Small-Scale Industry Delegation (1977), and Wong (1989) discuss Chinese rural industry before the reforms. Byrd and Lin (1990) and Wong (1988) discuss Chinese rural industry after the reforms.

In this paper, rural industry refers to privately-owned and collectively-owned rural enterprises. According to official statistics, among the different ownership patterns of Chinese rural industry, township-village collectively-owned enterprises (TVEs) are dominant, both in terms of labor employed, the amount of capital stock, and in terms of output. The ownership of most TVEs is not well-defined. A large proportion of TVEs are owned collectively and controlled jointly by individual entrepreneurs and the community governments.

Economists, observers, policy-makers, and politicians have different and controversial views on evaluating the growth and role of TVEs. With respect to efficiency, some believe that TVEs are more efficient than state-owned enterprises because they are market-oriented   and   have   more   economic   autonomy. Accordingly, the rapid growth of TVEs improves the efficiency of the national economy. The policy implications of this view is to encourage the fast growth of TVEs.[1]

Those who disagree with this view argue that TVEs are less efficient   than   state-owned   enterprises,   because   they   are small-scale and have more backward technology. The TVEs also suffer from the major disadvantage of state-sector enterprises, i.e., they are also controlled by local governments. According to this view, TVEs compete with the state sectors for raw materials, financial credits, and markets. Thus, the growth of TVEs is at the expense of the state-owned enterprises.[2]

Some field research and sample surveys of TVEs have been conducted. Because of methodological problems and limits on the scale of the research or surveys,[3] many results contradict each other, and thus can be used to support either view.

Systematic   econometric   analysis   may   be   helpful   to understand the relative efficiency of TVEs and state-owned enterprises. However, the only estimates for the growth rate of the total factor productivity (TFP) of TVEs in the literature are based on data from four counties.[4] Since there are no comparable studies available for state-owned enterprises in the same four counties, the results cannot be used to test the views even for these four counties. At the national level, several econometric investigations have been done to estimate the growth rate of the TFP for state-owned enterprises (Chen, Dernberger, the World Bank). However, there has not yet been any work to estimate the growth rate of the TFP for TVEs at the same level of aggregation over administrative units. Thus no comparisons can be made. This paper is the first endeavor in the literature to fill this gap. Because of data limitations, only the TVE sector is investigated quantitatively. With respect to other aspects of the TVEs, an institutional analysis is provided in the next section.

With regard to the development of TVEs in different regions

of China, the predominant view is that TVEs in "developed" regions (e.g. suburban regions[5] and coastal regions) are more efficient than TVEs in "underdeveloped" regions (e.g. the interior regions).[6] Views on this subject are important both to understand the operation of TVEs and also for policy implications. This paper is the first econometric study which tests TVE performance in different regions. It finds that in the most developed Chinese rural areas -- the suburban regions -- the growth rate of the total factor productivity for TVEs is the lowest among all regions. However, the level of the TFP for TVEs in suburban regions is the highest for all regions.

As for the behavior of TVEs, there are three contending views: (i) TVEs basically operate in a market environment, and a substantial proportion of resources are allocated by the markets according to profit maximization principles; (ii) TVEs are basically controlled by township and village governments, and thus bureaucratic control is dominant in the resource allocations of TVEs; (iii) TVEs are similar to labor-managed firms.

This paper investigates the employment behavior of TVEs using provincial data. I find that the wages of TVE employees are not determined by competitive labor markets -- the correlation between TVE wages and marginal products of labor is very weak, and TVE wages as well as the hypothetical worker income[7] are significantly lower than the marginal product of labor. These findings suggest that under bureaucratic control, the TVEs may be very different from profit-maximizing firms which operate in competitive markets and also may be quite different from labor-managed firms. Another interesting and puzzling phenomenon found in this paper is that of the labor shortage in the TVE sector, even though a labor surplus is a general problem in most Chinese rural areas.

The rest part of this chapter is organized as follows: In section 1, the institutional background and basic facts regarding the growth of TVEs are presented. Section 2 discusses data issues. In section 3, the methodology and estimation procedure are discussed. Section 4 presents the empirical results. Section 5 further discusses the behavior of TVEs. Section 6 discusses the productivity of TVEs and compares it with that of state-owned enterprises and with those in other countries.

1.INSTITUTIONAL BACKGROUND

1.1 The Growth and Institutional Evolution of TVEs

The predecessors of the TVEs were commune-brigade enterprises (CBE), which were owned and controlled by communes and brigades. In 1984, after the dissolution of the people's commune system, the CBEs were renamed township-village enterprises (TVEs). The growth of rural collective enterprises (CBEs and TVEs) from 1957 to 1988 is shown in Table 1 and Figure 1. To understand the strange growth pattern (large fluctuations and extraordinary growth after the mid-1970s), a brief introduction to the institution of TVEs is necessary.

The CBEs were initiated in 1958. In that year, the people's communes were established in China. The people's communes played a dual role in the rural areas: they were both the lowest government apparatus and the highest level of the rural collective system. The commune itself was organized hierarchically -- as the immediate subordinate units of the commune, there were brigades, and at the bottom level of the collective hierarchy, there were production teams. The budgets of communes and brigades mainly came from the CBEs. Therefore, the communes and brigades had very strong incentives to set up CBE.[8]

Table 1. Growth of TVE Output, 1957-1988.
(billion yuan) At 1980 constant prices.

Year	Output	Year	Output	Year	Output
1957	2.79	1971	11.1	1980	73.2
1958	6.91	1972	13.5	1981	83.0
1960	2.17	1973	15.5	1982	95.0
1961	2.08	1974	18.5	1983	112.9
1962	0.79	1975	23.7	1984	186.1
1963	0.40	1976	30.4	1985	294.9
1964	0.46	1978	55.0	1986	375.3
1965	0.55	1979	61.2	1987	474.3
				1988	627.3

Sources: 1957 to 1976: *Chinese Agricultural Yearbook, 1986.*
1978 to 1987: *Statistical Yearbook of China, 1988.*
1988: Renmin Ribao (Oversee's edition), Feb.28, 1989.

National retail price indexes from 1957 to 1987 are used, and the indexes are from *Statistical Yearbook of China, 1988.*

Price indexes for 1958, 1960, 1961, 1963, 1964, 1971, 1972, 1973, 1974 are interpolated values, and the price index for 1988 is an extrapolated value.

Under the control of the bureaucratic hierarchy, the life and death of the CBEs was determined to a great extent by government policy. According to Mao's goal of accelerating the pace of industrialization and speeding the transformation into a communist society, the central government launched a campaign to "run industry by the masses" as part of the People's Commune Campaign and the Great Leap Forward Campaign. During these campaigns, CBEs grew rapidly. In 1958, total employment of CBEs was 18 million and the gross value of CBE products was 6 billion yuan.[9] However, during the mass movements, without markets and without rigorous bureaucratic rules, many products from CBEs were useless except as accounting figures. Following the failure of the Great Leap Forward Campaign, and facing extremely severe shortages, the central government decided to shut down most CBEs. From 1960 to 1963, the number of CBEs dropped from 117,000 to 11,000, the gross value of CBE products fell from 1.98 billion yuan to 0.42 billion yuan. CBE growth began anew with the recovery of the economy. In the late 1960s, the CBEs had recovered to their level of the late 1950s.

During the Cultural Revolution (1966-1976), the central government policies which had a direct influence on the CBEs were those of "learn from Dazhai,"[10] "walk by two legs,"[11] and "farm mechanization." During this period, tens of thousands of small SOEs and county COEs[12] were set up. The growth of local small SOEs and urban COEs accumulated human capital and made it easier for the rural sector to boost industrial output both in the form of technology and in terms of producer goods. Much of the financial allocations for farm mechanization went to setting up CBEs.[13] On the other hand, "learn from Dazhai" further eliminated markets. CBEs were controlled tighter than before. After 1974, due to the many power struggles in the central government, central government control over local issues was substantially relaxed. Many local governments (e.g. in Jiangsu province) took advantage of this and set up enterprises which they could control directly and from which they could benefit. CBEs grow quickly since the mid-1970s. In 1976, at the end of the Cultural Revolution, the number of CBEs was 1.1 million, employment was 17.9 million, and gross output was 27.2 billion yuan.[14]

After 1978, accompanied with the economic reforms in the agricultural sector, central government policy toward CBEs changed dramatically by encouraging CBEs and relaxing central and provincial government controls, in order to raise efficiency and solve employment problems in the rural areas. In 1979, the

State Council issued the "Provisional Regulations on the Growth of CBEs."[15]

In the regulation, the most important policies benefiting the CBEs are: (a) to permit and encourage the growth of CBEs; (b) to give CBEs more autonomy in production and marketing decisions; (c) to prohibit the incorporation or transformation of CBEs into SOEs; (d) to reduce or abolish taxation of CBEs; and (e) to encourage SOEs to help and cooperate with CBEs.

Under these policies, from 1978 to 1987, the employment of TVEs increased at an annual rate of 15.2 percent (from 28.26 million in 1978 to 87.76 million in 1987), the number of TVEs increased at an annual rate of 35.7 percent (from 1.52 million to 17.45 million), and the total output of TVEs increased at an annual rate of 32.7 percent (from 49.3 billion to 474.3 billion).[16]

Because of the rapid growth of TVEs, the status of TVEs in the national economy changed from that of a subsidiary agricultural sector to a major sector. From 1976 to 1988, in terms of current prices, gross value of TVE products increased from 27.2 billion yuan, which accounted for 19.7 percent of the gross rural products (GRP),[17] to 642. billion yuan, which accounted for 53.5 percent of GRP.[18] From 1976 to 1987, total employment of TVEs increased from 17.9 million, which accounted for 5.9 percent of the total labor force in rural areas, to 87.76 million, which accounted for 22.5 percent of total labor force in the rural areas[19]. Concerning the industrial sector of TVEs (according to official statistics, there are industry, construction, construction material, transportation, service and agriculture sectors for TVEs), in 1987, total industrial production of TVEs was 324.3 billion yuan which accounted for 25.6 percent of the gross national industrial production.[20]

Table 2 shows the share of rural industry products in Chinese economy in 1988. As defined above, rural industry here combines the formal private sector and the TVE sector. From Table 2 we can see that rural industry is a major sector in the Chinese economy, especially in construction, material, and transportation sectors, where about 60 percent of the products or services nationwide were supplied by rural industry in 1987/1988.

1.2. Ownership

The phenomenal growth of Chinese rural industry was neither planned nor expected by the Chinese government. Deng Xiaoping himself recognized in 1988 that the amazing growth of rural industry was completely unexpected and was the greatest achievement of the reforms. Rural industry grew spontaneously whenever the government relaxed its policies against it. This spontaneous and spectacular growth is closely related to the growth of private ownership.

According to the official definition, the Chinese rural industry sector consists of TVEs (township-village enterprises) and PEs (private enterprises). By definition, TVEs are collectively-owned enterprises. However, the ownership of most TVEs is not at all clear. In terms of right of control, very often TVEs are tightly controlled by township and village governments. Thus, by and large, people regard TVEs as community government-run enterprises. Meanwhile, community governments view TVEs which are under their control as their own enterprises. However, the right to appropriate the assets of the TVEs is very vague. Some TVEs are owned neither by community governments nor owned by the collectives. But they are claimed to be collectively-owned. These TVEs are actually initiated and managed by individual entrepreneurs, and the property rights are not at all clear, since initially the entrepreneurs got authorization or help from the community

Table 2. Share of Rural Industrial Products
in the Chinese Economy, 1988.

Item	Share in the Nation
Total Output(a	
Total social products	24
Total rural social products	58
Total Industrial Output(a	28
Construction Material(b	
Total Value	59.7
Cement	24.8
Bricks	95.8
Construction	
Total Value(a	28.6
Completed Construction Area(b	40
Transportation(a	
Total Quantity	70.2
Total Value	58.4
Clothing(b	50.4
Mech. & Elect. Machinery(c	28.3
Mining(b	
Total Real Output	28
Coal	31
Textile(b	26

(a: Guan Zhiguo et al.

(b: Data for 1987: Chen Yaobang et al.

(c: Data for 1987: National data is from the State Statistical Bureau and TVP data is from Chen Yaobang et al.

Sources:

Guan Zhiguo et al. (ed), *Zhongguo Xiangzhen Qiye Gaikuang (Outline of Chinese TVPs)*. Beijing: Agriculture Press, 1989.

Chen Yaobang et al. (eds.), *Zhongguo Xiangzhen Qiye Nianjian*

(Yearbook   of Chinese TVPs), 1978-87. Beijing: Agriculture
Press, 1989.

State Statistical Bureau, *Statistical Yearbook of China, 1989.*
Beijing: Chinese Statistical Press, 1989.

government and/or state-owned enterprises to use land and to get
bank loans. To continue the special relationship with the
community government,   they claimed their enterprises to be
collectively-owned enterprises. However, very often, the value of
the TVE assets far exceed the value the entrepreneurs borrowed
from the government or from the state enterprises.
And many do not know who is the real owner of the assets.
Given the powerful position of the community governments in
affecting financial support, allocating energy and capital goods,
and the discouragement of government policies for privately-
owned enterprises (PEs) (especially before 1984), many PEs
claim to be TVEs.

  After 1984, the formal private sector has grown even faster
than the TVE sector. According to official sources, from 1984 to
1988, output of household-run enterprises increased 91.3 percent
annually, and output of partnership enterprises increased 45.1
percent annually. As a   result, in 1988, almost one-third of the
output of the township-village-private (TVP) sector was produced
by private enterprises. In about one-third of the provinces, such
as Hebei, Inner Mongolia, Jilin,   Heilongjiang, Anhui, Henan,
Guangxi, Hainan etc., the total output of PEs exceeded the total
outputs of the TVEs.

  Table 3 compares the TVE sector with the PE sector. The
quasi-private ownership may play a positive role in promoting
TVEs, but bureaucratic control is still a major feature and overall
may play a negative role in the TVE sector.

Table 3. Collectively and Privately-owned Rural Enterprises

	Enterprise(mil)		Empl'nt(mil)		Output(bil yuan)	
	TVE(a	PE(b	TVE(a	PE(b	TVE(a	PE(b
1978	1.52	-	28.3	-	49.3	-
1980	1.42	-	30.0	-	65.7	-
1984	1.86	4.21	39.8	12.3	146.6	24.4
1985	1.85	10.37	43.3	26.5	204.9	67.9
1986	1.73	13.42	45.4	34.0	251.6	102.4
1987	1.58	15.91	47.2	40.9	323.7	152.7
1988	1.59	17.29	48.9	46.5	436.3	213.3

(a: TVE includes township and village enterprises.
(b: PE includes household-run enterprises and partnership enterprises.

Source: Guan Zhiguo et al. (eds.), *Zhongguo Xiangzhen Qiye Gaikuang (Outline of Chinese TVPs)*. Beijing: Agriculture Press, 1989.

Although control by the central and provincial governments was relaxed after 1978, the central government still insisted on its primary position of public (local government)[21] ownership and public (local government) control over the CBEs. From the regulations, one can see that in name CBEs are collective, but in reality they are controlled by commune (township) and brigade (village) governments. According to the regulations of 1979, "CBEs are socialist collectively-owned enterprises. Commune enterprises are owned by communes, and brigade enterprises are owned by brigades." The regulations emphasize the importance of controlling the operation of CBEs through the local government bureaucracy. It reads that "planning committees and government agencies at all levels of government, especially industrial agencies, should not only take care of SOEs, but also take care of CBEs. They should adopt all possible measures to strengthen the production, supply, and sales plans of CBEs."[22]

In 1984, the people's communes were disbanded, and the CBEs were renamed TVEs by the central government. Most major policies on CBEs stipulated in the 1979 regulations were basically unchanged. The TVEs were largely controlled by township (former commune) and village (former brigade) governments.

Many scholars in China argue that under this institutional arrangement -- i.e. local government control -- TVEs are similar to SOEs in the following respects: (i) TVEs are actually affiliated units of the Party and government apparatuses in the rural areas; (ii) TVEs do not have genuine autonomy in business transactions; (iii) with regard to the control of TVEs, there is no separation between government and enterprise; (iv) the arrangement of managerial personnel and employment is basically determined by the Party committees.[23] Field research done by the Central Committee Secretariat and the State Council found that "in the institution of TVEs, it is very common to see that the basic rights (of TVEs) are in the hands of the Party and (local) government apparatus, i.e. TVEs are not genuine cooperative enterprises. A significant portion of the net profits (of TVEs) is used for the administrative budget of the TV governments."[24]

Township and village governments simultaneously play a role as administrators and owners. Therefore, once the central government allows township and village governments to set up enterprises, they always take advantage of their administrative power to foster their own enterprises -- TVEs. As administrators, township governments have the power to allocate capital goods at low official prices. They deliberately give benefits to the township enterprises through this channel.[25]

In addition to the benefits and protection provided by governments, TVEs are also controlled and restricted by governments. According to a sample survey, 83.3 percent of township enterprise directors thought that they were appointed by the township government; 71.9 percent of the directors felt that decisions on worker recruitment were made by the township government; and 71.9 percent thought that the proportion of profits that the TE could retain was determined by the township government.[26]

To understand many features related to the growth and behavior of TVEs, a special institutional arrangement called the *"hukou zhidu (household registration system),"* which had been effective until the mid-1980s, should be presented here. The household registration system is an institutional arrangement which fundamentally affects the motivation to set up TVEs and the fundamental efficiency of TVEs. This system prevented migration. Most families in rural communities have remained in the same communities for generations. Restrictions on migration result only in the immobility of human resources but also in the immobility of capital. Since under this system the welfare of the rural population relies almost completely on the prosperity of the village or township, people from the head of the township down to common residents regard the prosperity of their township as their primary concern, and they are unwilling to share their gains with surrounding communities.

2.DATA

The estimates and results obtained in this paper are based on official data. In view of the availability and consistency of the data, this paper focuses on township-village collectively-owned enterprises (commune-brigade enterprises before 1984). In principle, the data are constructed in accordance with the standard national income accounting conventions and were collected using comprehensive statistical forms through an administrative hierarchy.

For the estimation of production functions, data for output, capital, and labor are required.

All relevant official Chinese data are published at current prices. To convert output indexes and capital indexes from current prices to constant prices, price indexes are needed. Given the fact that all TVEs are very small and most of their output is sold in markets, retail price indexes[27] are used in this paper.

Output indexes Y_{it} are constructed from official Chinese statistics on TVE output and from official price indexes.[28] Y_{it} is deflated from the output of TVEs at current prices to constant 1980 prices.

Capital indexes Y_{it} are also from official Chinese sources. The ideal capital index in estimating production functions would be the annual flow of capital services. However, there is no reliable information on capital utilization or on the real rate of return on capital. The only alternative is the net value of the capital stock ("net value of fixed assets" in official Chinese sources). In this paper, fixed asset figures are also deflated from current prices to constant 1980 prices. Unlike state-owned enterprises, in general TVEs do not provide housing to their employees. Thus there is no need to remove "non-productive capital" from the fixed asset data.[29] The major possible problems in simply using fixed asset data as a measure of capital input are the following: (i) this implicitly assumes that capital utilization is the same for all TVEs in all regions. Actually this is not the case. According to reports of many field researchers, the most serious problem which affects capital utilization is energy and raw material supplies (in many areas, capital is utilized at only two-thirds of its potential because of the lack of electricity). The situation is usually worse for those TVEs which do not have a strong relationship with the township or village governments. Therefore, this kind of assumption may result in an overestimation of capital productivity for those TVEs with better energy supplies and an underestimation of capital productivity for those TVEs with worse energy supplies. However, without reliable detailed direct or indirect information on the utilization of capital, there is no way to adjust the data.

(ii) The Chinese convention of calculating the current year's fixed assets is to add the value of the previous year's capital at original prices and the fixed assets added in the current year at current prices, and subtract the capital depreciation at current prices. Therefore, the so-called fixed assets at current prices are actually a weighted summation of capital stock, where the weights are the prices of all the previous years. Prices are not stable, and the rate of capital depreciation is arbitrarily determined by the bureaucracies. Price distortions of producer goods is another major problem. These errors can be in any direction. Without further information, it is impossible to correct them.

(iii) When comparing TVEs with state-owned enterprises, it should be noted that some of the TVE capital goods are purchased from markets at prices higher than the official allocation prices, at which state-owned enterprises get their capital goods. On the other hand, some of the TVE capital goods are obtained at very low prices from state-owned enterprises with which they have special mutual benefit relationships.

Labor indexes Y_{it} are also from official Chinese sources. The ideal labor index to estimate the production functions would be a measure of the labor hours used in production process. Without detailed information on labor utilization, we are forced to use employment as an alternative, which results in the assumption that labor utilization is the same in all TVEs and in all regions. Labor utilization also varies among different TVEs and different regions. The variations are not only caused by shortages of energy and raw material, but also by agricultural seasonality (e.g., in the peak season the number of people who work in TVEs is less than in other seasons).

The data used in estimating growth and productivity appear in the Appendix.

For the testing of the hypotheses on the behavior of TVEs, the following data are needed: average TVE wages, SOE wages, COE wages.

From official sources, data on total wage bills and total employment of TVEs, COEs and SOEs are available. In this paper, all wages are deflated to 1980 prices.

3.METHODOLOGY

(1) Growth and Productivity

Aggregate production functions are used to investigate the growth and productivity of TVEs. The basic assumptions in the specification of the production functions are the following: (i)

Hicks-neutral, disembodied technical change or total factor productivity change; (ii) constant elasticity of substitution.

The questions related to the growth and productivity of TVEs to be answered in this part of the paper are the following: (i) what is the contribution of the total factor productivity (TFP) change to the growth of TVE output?; (ii) is the growth rate of TFP in the TVE sector increasing, constant, or decreasing over time?; (iii) how can we explain different growth rates of TVEs in different regions of China?

To answer these questions, and to find a specification which best fits the data, the following hypotheses need to be tested: hypothesis one (H1) -- elasticities of labor and capital are different across regions; hypothesis two (H2) -- elasticities of labor and capital are constant over time; hypothesis three (H3) -- total factor productivity is different across regions; hypothesis four (H4) -- total factor productivity is constant over time; and hypothesis five (H5), elasticity of substitution is one.

Under the assumptions of Hicksian neutral TFP and constant elasticity of substitution, the following CES production function is specified:

$$\ln Y_{it} A(t) - v/\rho \ln [\delta K_{it}^{-\rho} + (1-\delta)L_{it}^{-\rho}] + \varepsilon_{it}$$

If $\rho = 0$, then the CES function is reduced to the following Cobb-Douglas function.

$$\ln Y_{it} = A(t) + \beta \ln K_{it} + \alpha \ln L_{it} + \varepsilon_{it}.$$

The terms are defined as follows:
t = time in years;
i = province i;
Y_{it} an index of the value of net product (value-added) in province i at time t, evaluated at 1980 prices;
K_{it} value of net capital stock of TVEs in province i during year t at 1980 prices;
L_{it} the number of workers of TVEs in province i during year t;

ε_{it} = error in province i during year t. I assume that error ε_{it} is identically independently distributed;

δ = factor distribution coefficient;

v = scale return coefficient;

ρ = substitution coefficient. elasticity of substitution = $1/(1-\rho)$;

α = output elasticity with respect to labor input;

β = output elasticity with respect to capital input.

To test H1, regional dummies are created for elasticities. If there are no significant differences among elasticities in different regions, H1 will be rejected. The regional dummies are: suburban region, coastal region, and interior region.[30]

To test H2, elasticities are allowed to vary over time and are approximated by a linear equation, e.g., output-labor elasticity can be specified as $\alpha + \alpha't$. If α' is not significantly different from zero for all regions, output-labor elasticity should be considered constant over time. Concerning possible differences in regions, regional dummies are created as well.

To test H3, we again create regional dummies when estimating the growth rate of the TFP. If there are significant differences among the estimated growth rates of the TFP for different regions, H3 cannot be rejected.

To test H4, the TFP growth rate is approximated by the following linear relationship: $\lambda_1 + \lambda_2 t$. If λ_2 is not significantly different from zero, then H4 cannot be rejected.

To test H5, a CES function is estimated. If the estimated substitution elasticity is not significantly different from one, H5 cannot be rejected, and the Cobb-Douglas function is the proper specification of the technology.

In the estimations, the following specifications of the production functions are used. First, the Kmenta approximation[31] of CES function with time-variable TFP, time-variable factor distribution coefficients and regional dummies is specified as follows:

$$\ln Y_{it} = \bar{a}D + (\bar{\lambda}_1 + \bar{\lambda}_2 t)Dt + v(\bar{\delta} + \bar{\delta}'t)D\ln K_{it}$$

$$+ v(1-(\bar{\delta}+\bar{\delta}'t)D \ln L_{it}$$

$$- 0.5pv(\bar{\delta}+\bar{\delta}'t)(1-(\bar{\delta}+\bar{\delta}'t))D (\ln(K_{it}/L_{it}))^2+\varepsilon_{it} \qquad (CES1)$$

Here, $D = (D_{city}, D_{coast}, D_{inter})$ = vector of dummy variables for the three greater regions: city stands for suburban region, coast for coastal region, and inter for interior region; $\bar{a} = (a_{city}, a_{coast}, a_{inter})$ = vector of intercepts for the three regions; $\bar{\lambda}_1$ and $\bar{\lambda}_2 = (\lambda_{j,city}, \lambda_{j,coast}, \lambda_{j,inter})$ = vectors of coefficients of the growth rates of the TFP for the three regions, j = 1,2. For each region, the growth rate of the TFP is $\lambda_1+ \lambda_2 t$; $\bar{\delta}'= (\delta'_{city}, \delta'_{coast}, \delta'_{inter})$ = vector of the growth rate of factor distribution for the three regions.

If the substitution elasticity is restricted to one, the CES-1 is reduced to a Cobb-Douglas function with time variable TFP, time variable elasticities of input factors and regional dummies, which is specified as follows:

$$\ln Y_{it} = \bar{a}D + (\bar{\lambda}_1+\bar{\lambda}_2t)Dt + (\bar{\alpha}+\bar{\alpha}'t)D \ln L_{it} + (\bar{\beta}+\bar{\beta}'t))D \ln K_{it} = \varepsilon_{it} \qquad (CD\text{-}1)$$

Testing the hypotheses step by step, the best estimated equation is the following:

$$\ln Y_{it} = \bar{a}D +(\bar{\lambda}_1+\lambda_2t)Dt + \alpha \ln L_{it} + \beta \ln K_{it} + \varepsilon_{it} \quad (CD\text{-}6)$$

Other specifications which are used in the estimation procedure appear in the Appendix.

(2) TVE Behavior

In this subsection, TVE behavior is studied by investigating employment and wage determination in the TVE sector.

Given the fact that all TVEs are small in scale, if TVEs are profit-maximizing firms operating in competitive labor markets, one should observe the wages of TVE employees to be equal to their marginal product. If TVEs are labor-managed firms, then workers' income should be equal to the marginal product of labor. Suppose all profits are distributed to workers of TVEs; the workers' hypothetical income should then be their wages plus all profits.[32] Therefore, if TVEs are labor-managed firms, the following relationship should hold: $Itve_{it} = Wtve_{it} + \pi_{it}/L_{it} = MPL_{it}$. Here, $Itve_{it}$ and π_{it} are hypothetical workers' income and the profit of TVEs in province i during year t, respectively.

Based on the estimated production function, the marginal product of labor of TVEs in province i during year t can be estimated in the following way:

$$MPL_{it} = \partial Y_{it}/\partial L_{it} = \alpha_{it}$$

Given the institutions of Chinese rural areas, the autonomy of TVEs may be limited. That is, wage determination in the TVE sector may be affected by egalitarian rules and/or other rules formulated and enforced through administrative channels.

A possible rule is an egalitarian rule imposed by the community governments. If TVE wages are completely determined according to this rule within the rural communities which run them, then all incomes from TVEs should be distributed equally to all the members of the communities.[33] In this situation, the wages of TVE workers will be the same as (or close to) the incomes of rural laborers in the community. Thus a comparison of the wages of the TVEs and the incomes of rural laborers in the same locality can be used as a measurement of the influence of egalitarianism on wage determination within the communities.

Another possible situation is that the wages of TVEs are determined according to policies which are formulated by the central government. A typical wage-policy for collectively-owned enterprises is that COEs and TVEs need to consult the standard wage-ranking of the SOEs, which are stipulated by the central government. Thus, in the extreme situation, TVE-wages are the same as SOE-wages or COE-wages. In general, as long as this kind of policy plays an important role, TVE-wages should be highly correlated with COE-wages.

To test the hypotheses on TVE wage determination, the following nested estimation equation -- wage equation -- is specified:

$$W_{tve_{it}} = a + b \, MPL_{it} + b' \, \pi_{it}/L_{it}$$

$$+ c \, W_{coe_{it}} + d \, W_{ag_{it}} + \varepsilon_{it} \qquad (W\text{-}1)$$

$$W_{tve_{it}} = a + b \, MPL_{it} + b' \, \pi_{it}/L_{it}$$

$$+ c' \, W_{soe_{it}} + d \, W_{ag_{it}} + \varepsilon_{it} \qquad (W\text{-}2)$$

Here, $W_{ag_{it}}$ = average income of rural laborers in province i in year t; $W_{tve_{it}}$= average wage of TVE employees in province i in year t; $W_{coe_{it}}$= average wage of urban collectively-owned enterprises (COE) employees in province i during year t; $W_{soe_{it}}$= average wage of urban state-owned enterprise (SOE) employees in province i during year t; a, b, b', c, c', d are coefficients to be estimated.

If $a = b' = c = d = 0$ and $b = 1$, then the wages of TVE employees are completely determined by competitive labor markets and TVEs are profit-maximizing firms; if $a = c = c' = d = 0$, $b = 1$ and $b' = -1$, then the incomes of TVE workers are determined completely by competitive labor markets and TVEs are labor-managed firms;[34] and if $a = b = d = 0$ and $d = 1$, then W_{tve} is equally distributed in the rural communities; if $a = b = c = 0$ and $c = 1$ ($c' = 1$), then the rules of wage determination in the TVEs are completely the same as those of urban COEs (SOEs).

4.EMPIRICAL RESULTS

(1) Growth and Productivity

The following procedure was used to identify the best specification: (1) CES-1 was estimated. Since the estimated substitution elasticity is not significantly different from one, H5 cannot be rejected. In the following, except for the last step, only CD functions were estimated.

(2) CD-1 to CD-4 were estimated. According to the results, the elasticities of labor and capital are statistically the same across regions. Thus H1 is rejected.

(3) According to the estimation of CD-5, changes in the growth rate of the TFP are not significantly different across regions. In other words, λ_2 is the same for all three regions.

(4) CD-6 was estimated. The results show that the elasticities of the input factors are constant over the period. Thus H2 is accepted.

(5) I estimated CD-7, which is a restricted version of CD-6. The results show that the growth rates of the TFP are significantly different across regions, or λ_1 is different across regions. Thus H3 is accepted.

(6) CD-8 was estimated, which is another restricted version of CD-6. According to the estimation, λ_2 is significantly different from zero, i.e. $(\lambda_1 + \lambda_2 t)$ is a better expression of the TFP growth than λ_1. So H4 is rejected.

(7) CES-2, which is the CES function counterpart of CD-6, was estimated. Again, the estimated substitution elasticity is not significantly different from one (ρ is not significant

Table 4. Estimated Production Functions of TVEs

	CD-6 Coef. SE	CD-8 Coef. SE	CD-9 Coef. SE	CES-2 Coef. SE
Dcity	-.910 .170	-.867 .172	-.91 .161	.082 .085
Dcoast	-1.35 .176	-1.32 .179	-1.19 .174	-.354 .062
Dinter	-1.48 .162	-1.44 .164	-1.43 .166	-.483 .0525
Tcity	.135 .0354	.063 .0194	-	.135 .0357
Tcoast	.182 .0320	.110 .0127	-	.182 .0324
Tinter	.149 .0314	.076 .0084	-	.149 .0320
t	- -	-	.083 .0072	-
t^2	-.011 .0044	-	-.011 .0045	
β	.484 .0558	.445 .0542	.465 .0539	-
α	.573 .0536	.611 .0520	.591 .0552	-
δ	-	-	-	.456 .0534
ρ	-	-	-	1.06 .0114
ν	-	-	-	.14 1.10
$\bar{R}^2$	.989	.988	.988	.989
DW	1.77	1.72	1.67	1.77
SSR	2.97	3.07	3.21	2.97
Obser	168	168	168	168

Dcity, Dcoast, and Dinter are the intercepts for the three regions;

Tcity, Tcoast, and Tinter are the constant terms of the TFP growth for the three regions;
t is the constant term of the TFP growth;
t^2 is the first order term of the TFP growth;
β and α are the output elasticities of capital and labor respectively;
δ, ν and ρ are the factor distribution coefficient, scale coefficient, and substitution coefficient respectively.

different from zero and the substitution elasticity $\sigma = 1/(1-\rho)$). H6 is rejected. In addition, the coefficient of return to scale ν is significantly different from one, i.e. there is a significant increasing return to scale.

(8) The whole estimation procedure concludes that CD-6 is the best specification.

CD-6 and its CES counterpart CES-2 appear in Table 4. CD-8 and a more restricted version of the CD functions are also shown in Table 4.

The major findings can be summarized as follows:

(1) According to estimated CD-6, the growth rate of the TFP in the TVE sector is high, but the growth rate is decreasing at about one percent per year. If this trend continues, in less than fifteen years (beginning from 1982), the growth rate of TFP in TVE sector will be near zero.

(2) According to the estimates of CD-6 and CD-8, the growth rate of the TFP in the coastal region is the highest in the nation, which is (18.2 - 1.08 t) percent in CD-6, or 11 percent in CD-8. Here, t is the year beginning from 1982. The growth rate of TFP in the suburban region is the lowest in the nation, which is (13.5 - 1.08 t) percent in CD-6, or 6.28 percent in CD-8; the growth rate of the TFP in the most underdeveloped region -- the interior region -- is higher than in the suburban region which is the most developed region in China: the growth rate is (14.9 - 1.08 t) percent in CD-6, or 7.57 percent in CD-8.

(3) According to the estimation of CES-2, the elasticity of input factor substitution in the TVE sector is one, and thus a Cobb-Douglas production function best fits the data.

(4) Statistically, the elasticities of labor and capital are the same across regions. Also, during the period under examination, the elasticities are constant over time. The labor elasticity is 0.573, and the capital elasticity is 0.484.

(2) Behavior of TVEs

The estimated results of wage equations W-1 and W-2 appear in Table 5. The major findings can be summarized as follows:

(i) The marginal product of labor in the TVE sector is weakly correlated with the TVE wages. Thus, competitive labor markets play little role in determining the TVE wage or hypothetical worker income. Therefore, the hypothesis that TVEs are profit-maximizing and that they operate in competitive markets can be rejected.

(ii) The coefficient of per-worker profit is significantly greater than zero. Combining this with result (i), the hypothesis that TVEs are labor-managed firms is rejected.

(iii) The correlation between TVE wages and urban collectively-owned enterprises (COE) or state-owned enterprises (SOE) wages is very strong. Combining this with (i) and (ii), it raises the possibility that TVEs do not determine their employment and wages autonomously. Instead, for wage determination, they may have to adopt partly the wage-ranking standard in urban COEs (SOEs), which is set by governments;[35] in employment, there may exist administrative restrictions,[36] which force TVEs to hire laborers at a point away from the one where the marginal product of labor equals the given exogenous wage.

(iv) The correlation between rural laborers' incomes and TVE wages is significant. Combining this with (i) and (ii), it suggests that the principle of equal distribution within communities where TVEs are located does play a role in wage determination.

Table 5. Estimated Wage Equations

	W-1 Coef. SE		W-2 Coef. SE	
Intercept	163.0	57.4	177.4	61.1
Wcoe	.352	.0847	-	
Wsoe	-		.215	.0596
π/L	.227	.0729	.222	.0741
MPL	.022	.0139	.0312	.0134
$\overline{W}$ag	.106	.0625	.146	.0640
$\overline{R}^2$	.572		.557	
DW	1.61		1.70	

Wcoe and Wsoe are COE wages and SOE wages respectively; π/L is the profit per worker in TVEs; MPL is the marginal product of labor in TVEs; Wag is rural laborer income.

5. DISCUSSION OF TVE BEHAVIOR

To explain further the findings from the estimated wage equations, let us look at the marginal product of labor and wages directly.

The means and standard deviations of the estimated marginal products of labor, and of the TVE average wages, hypothetical TVE worker incomes, COE average wages, SOE average wages as well as the average rural laborer incomes are shown in Table

6. The data (from twenty-eight provincial areas from 1984 to 1987) from which the means and standard deviations are calculated are shown in the Appendix.

Comparing the MPLs with the average TVE wages, and with hypothetical TVE worker incomes, one can observe that: (i) from 1984 to 1987 in the twenty-eight provincial areas, the mean of the MPLs was 2.8 and 1.6 times higher than the mean of the TVE wages and the mean of the hypothetical worker incomes of TVEs respectively.

(ii) The gap between the MPLs and wages in the TVEs becomes larger over time. In 1984, the ratio between the mean of TVE MPLs and the mean of TVE wages was less than three. In 1987, the ratio increased to almost five.

(iii) The variation of MPLs is much larger than those of TVE wages and hypothetical worker incomes: the standard deviation of MPLs is 4.9 and 2.6 times higher than those of TVE wages and hypothetical worker incomes respectively.

(iv) There are regularities between the wages of TVEs and the wages of COEs (or SOEs) in their distribution across provinces and over time: TVE wages are always lower than COE (SOE) wages, and the gaps between COE (SOE) wages and TVE wages are not large -- never bigger than one-third of COE wages.

(v) The disparity between MPL and TVE wages varies irregularly across regions. For example, in 1987, in the most developed region -- suburban Shanghai -- the MPL was 5.6 times higher than the TVE wage. However, in the most underdeveloped region -- Guizhou -- the disparity between the MPL and TVE wages was the smallest in the nation: both the MPL of TVEs and rural laborer income in Guizhou were among the lowest of all provinces, but the wage of TVE workers in the province was higher than the average wage of TVEs at the national level. Consistent with the interpretation that TVE-wages are to a large extent determined by local governments, one can observe that COE wages (and SOE wages) in Guizhou are also higher than the national average, and that TVE wages basically follow this trend.[37]

One may interpret the above findings in terms of alternative wages. That is, because of the role of labor mobility or labor markets, COE wages or SOE wages serve as alternative wages for TVE employees, and therefore affect TVE wages. However, if TVEs are autonomous profit-maximizing firms or labor-managed firms, given exogenous alternative wages, they should hire laborers to the point where the marginal product of labor is equal to the exogenous alternative wage. With the marginal product of labor significantly higher than the wages, it is difficult to explain the rational for maintaining such a situation using this kind of interpretation.

Table 6. Means and Standard Deviations
of Wages and Marginal Products of Labor

		MPL	W_{tve}	I_{tve}	W_{coe}	W_{soe}	W_{ag}
84	Mean	1769	611	923	755	969	659
Stan. Dev		522	103	206	85	119	207
85	Mean	2301	638	967	792	1002	608
Stan. Dev		741	114	236	114	123	188
86	Mean	2616	654	944	834	1098	618
Stan. Dev		832	114	211	106	123	208
87	Mean	3186	664	964	897	1164	630
Stan. Dev		1090	150	256	132	139	224
84-87 Mean		2343	609	901	778	1005	596
Stan. Dev		1089	185	305	216	274	245

Means and standard deviations of the variables are calculated from the variables in twenty-eight provinces from 1984 to 1987, which appear in the Appendix.

In the table, MPL is the marginal product of labor in the TVEs; W_{tve} and I_{tve} are the TVE wage and the hypothetical TVE worker income respectively; W_{coe}, W_{soe}, and W_{ag} are the COE wage, SOE wage, and rural laborer income respectively.

Table 7. Decision making in Sample Township Enterprises

	Made by factory	Not made by factory	No response
Decisions regarding appointment of factory director	13.3	83.3	3.4
Formation of management team	50.0	40.0	10.0
Worker hiring	28.8	71.9	-
Large production expenditures	87.5	12.5	0
Production plan	50.0	18.8	31.2
Proportion of retained profits	19.4	71.9	8.7

Source: Enterprise Director Questionnaire. in Song Lina, "Convergence: A Comparison of Township-run Firms and Local State Enterprises," in Byrd and Lin (eds.) (1990).

There is much evidence from the field research which shows that, to a great extent, local governments do have an important influence over employment and wage determination in TVEs. In the World Bank field research, 83.3 percent of the TVE managers stated that their positions were determined by the government, and 71.9 percent of the TVE managers thought that worker recruitment was determined by the government. Table 7 suggests that employment policy and the proportion of profits submitted to local governments are the two issues about which the local governments most care. As their careers are influenced by governments, TVE managers follow the policies or rules for recruitment as suggested by local governments. In Shangrao county, researchers found that the government asked the TVEs to copy or to adopt the wage system of the SOEs.[38] In Wu Xi county, they found that the total wage bill of the TVEs was approved by the government. If the TVE total wages surpass the standard set by the government, extra taxes are levied on the relevant TVEs.[39]

Table 8. How Were Workers Hired by TVEs.
(% of total sample of workers in each county)

	Wuxi	Jieshou	Nanhai	Shangrao
Assigned by township or village government	56.8	15.5	38.0	44.4
Examinations	15.8	30.7	3.9	2.8
Applications	9.2	12.5	15.7	20.8
Fund raising	0.9	12.8	1.2	9.7
By recommendation	16.0	28.0	41.2	22.2
Other channels	0.6	0.3	0.0	0.0

Sources: Worker survey questionnaire in Meng Xin, "The Rural Labor Market," in Byrd and Lin (eds.) (1990).

Sample surveys of workers' view also present evidence that employment is influenced by the government. A sample survey by the Chinese Development Institute shows that 40.1 percent of TVE employees got their job directly through TV government assignment (at the setting-up stage, the percentage was 49).[40] The field research of the World Bank presents similar evidence. The results are shown in Table 8.

From Table 8 one can see that in the four counties, quite a large percentage of employees are assigned to their jobs by government. Still, there are many workers get jobs by passing examinations or through recommendations. For this portion of the work force, it is quite possible that their employment and wages are also influenced to a large extent by the local governments.

5.1 Labor Shortages in the TVE Sector

Another interesting explanation for the disparity between wages and the MPL is the labor shortage. It is well known that, in general, in Chinese rural areas, a labor surplus is a popular phenomenon. But the "household registration system" plus the grain procurement system and the low productivity of grain production may restrict migration and thus generate a local labor shortage problem even though in general there is a labor surplus.

Under the "household registration system," all "rural residents" are not eligible to buy foodstuffs in state-owned food stores, no matter whether their jobs are agricultural or nonagricultural. In state food stores, the prices of foodstuffs are low (because of low procurement prices and government subsidies) and the quantity which each urban resident can buy is guaranteed (since the government uses administrative or coercive force, e.g. it closes free markets for foodstuffs before their procurement target is achieved, to purchase grain at low official prices).[41] The low price for the "purchasing" of large quantities of grain provides low incentives for producing grain, thus in the free markets not only are prices of foodstuffs high but also supplies fluctuate very much.

To insure their food consumption, most TVE employees and their families have to keep their "responsibility land" and they have to do farm work on the land. They regard their land as insurance both in the sense of guaranteeing their food consumption and in the sense of their basic income. When they have troubles in the TVEs, they can always go home to do the farm work.

According to a sample survey of 900 rural laborers from nine counties in Henan province, 99.6 percent of the nonagricultural workers responded that their "responsibility land" was taken care of by their family members. Only 0.4 percent of them contract their land out to others. Regarding their preferences, 86 percent of the nonagricultural workers responded that they prefer to keep their land; and 91 percent of the agricultural workers said that they would like to find nonagricultural jobs. But if they had a nonagricultural job, they still would want to keep their land. Because, according to the response of 89 percent of the nonagricultural workers, if they have trouble or lose their jobs in the TVEs, they can go home to do farm work.[42] According to another survey in Yuanping county of Shanxi province, only 3.8 percent of the TVE employees do not have "responsibility land," and only 9 percent of them do no farm work on their "responsibility land" (62.8 percent of them do farm work in the busy seasons, and 28.2 percent of them frequently do farm work to supplement their production).[43] A nationwide sample survey of 3200 rural households in twenty-eight provinces and municipalities shows a similar result: 72.4 percent of the sample households prefer to keep the current "land responsibility system," they do not want more "responsibility land," nor do they want less land.[44] This shows that most rural people are not enthusiastic about agriculture, because income from agriculture is too low. However, they do not want to give up farm work either, because they need the insurance guarantees.

In many surveys, researchers find that while a labor shortage is a serious problem in relatively industrialized areas, in most rural areas the still abundant labor supply has not been fully utilized. In Yuanping county, which is a relatively industrialized area (only in the local sense), 47.4 percent of the TVPs reported that a labor shortage was a problem in their operations.[45]

6. PRODUCTIVITY COMPARISON

In this section, the TFP growth in the TVE sector from 1982 to 1987 is compared with China's state-owned sector and also with other economies. Three groups of estimates of the growth rate of the TFP in the TVE sector are shown in Table 9. The estimates of group C are the results of CD-6, which is the best specification according to my estimation procedure. Group A is from CD-9. The estimation of the TFP growth from CD-9 is the lowest among the estimates of all specifications. Thus the results can be used as a lower bound of the TFP growth rate in the TVE sector.

In Table 9, the growth rates of the TFP in the state-owned sector are from Chen,K., G.Jefferson, T.Rawski, H.Wang, and Y.Zheng (abbreviated as CJRWZ) (1988). In their paper, there are four methods for estimating the TFP growth rate: it is estimated directly from the production functions based on original data and revised data, and estimated from a TFP index based on original data and revised data. The TFP index used is the following: $Y/(\alpha L + \beta K)$; here, Y is a net output index, L and K are labor and capital input indexes, and α and β are output-labor and output-capital elasticities respectively. Theoretically, this index is problematic when it is used to measure changes in productivity.[46]

In making comparisons, it would make sense only when the measurement methods are the same. To avoid the problems with the index, and to make comparisons with other literature, the TFP growth rate estimated directly from the production function is preferred when comparing the productivity change of TVEs with that of SOEs.

Table 9. Comparison of Total Factor Productivity Growth

share output growth(%)		Output grow. rate (% p.a.)			TFP growth (% p.a.)		TFP of
		A	B	C	A	B	C
TVE 82-87							
Nation	26.0	8.3^a	8.4^b	12.5^c	31.9^a	32.3^b	48.1^c
Suburb	23.0		6.28^b	10.3^c		27.3^b	44.7^c
Coast	32.6		11.0^b	15.0^c		33.7^b	46.0^c
Interior	21.0		7.57^b	11.7^c		36.0^b	55.7^c
SOE 78-85^d		8.6	1.3^{d1}	0.5^{d2}	5.2^{d3}	15.0	.05860.4
USSR 60-70^g		1.5			29.0		
70-75^g		0.1			3.0		
Average for seven centrally planned economies^e		2.5			35.0		
Average for nineteen developing countries^e		2.0			31.0		
Average for twelve developed market economies^e		2.7			49.0		
Korea 60-73^f		4.1			42.0		
Japan 60-73^f		4.5			41.0		

a-d: are all estimated by the Cobb-Douglas production function, based on 1980 constant prices.

a: estimated by CD-9.

b: estimated by CD-8. The TFP growth rate at the national level is calculated by taking the weighted average of the TFP growth in three regions (weights are the number of provinces in each region).

c: estimated by CD-6. The TFP growth rate at the national level is calculated by taking weighted average of the TFP growth in three regions.

d: CJRWZ, (1988), "Productivity Change in Chinese Industry: 1953-1985." *Journal of Comparative Economics*, 12:570-591.
d1: estimated directly from the CD function by using revised data.
d2: estimated directly from the CD function by using original data.
d3: estimated from derived the TFP index by using revised data.

e: Chenery, H., et al. (eds.), (1986), *Industrialization and Growth: A Comparative Study*, New York: Oxford University Press, p.22.

f: Christensen, L., D.Cummings, and D.Jorgenson, (1980), "Economic Growth, 1947-73: An International Comparison," in J.Kendrick et al. (eds.) *New Developments in Productivity Measurement and Analysis,* NBER, The University of Chicago Press.

g: Bergson, A., and H.Levine (eds.), (1983), *The Soviet Economy Towards the Year 2000*, London. Chapter 2.

In CJRWZ's paper, "original data" refers to data from Chinese official sources, and "revised data" refers to data they have revised.[47] If the estimate based on the revised data is regarded as the upper limit of the growth rate of the TFP in the state sector, and the estimate based on original data is regarded as the lower limit of the growth rate, then the growth rate of the TFP in the state sector in 1978-85 is between 0.5 percent and 1.3 percent.[48]

Even using the lower limit of the TFP growth rate estimates for the TVE sector (1982-87) to compare with the upper limit of the TFP growth in the SOE sector and with the TFP growth rate in the USSR state sector, the TFP growth rate of TVEs is still much higher than the rate for China's state sector (1978-85) and the rate for the USSR state sector (1960-75). Comparing the share of the TFP change in the growth of output, the share in the TVE sector is also higher than the share in the Chinese state sector and the share in the USSR state sector.[49]

Compared to the economies which are not centrally-planned, the TFP growth rate of the Chinese TVE sector is higher than that in South Korea (1960-73) and Japan (1960-73), which have been among the highest in the world during the past two decades. According to the group C results, the share of the TFP growth in the growth of output in the Chinese TVE sector is similar to the share in South Korea and in Japan. According to the results of group A, the share in the Chinese TVE sector is similar to the share for average developing countries.

A possible explanation for the high growth rate of the TFP in the TVE sector is the following hypothesis: the fast growth of the TFP in the TVE sector is basically a result of low productivity in TVEs at the starting stage (for convenience, hereafter, I call this the "low starting stage" hypothesis), combined with technology transfer from other sectors to the TVE sector. At a very low level of productivity, by introducing technologies from other sectors, the TVEs can improve their productivity quickly. However, once the technology transfer is completed, or the TFP level gap between the TVE sector and the state sector disappears, the difference in the TFP growth rates between the TVE sector and the other sectors should also disappear.

Table 10. TFP Levels in the TVE sector(a

	Nation	Suburb	Coast	Inter
1982	2.32	3.34	2.55	1.89
1983	2.60	3.60	2.87	2.11
1984	2.86	3.80	3.09	2.40
1985	3.40	4.05	3.92	2.63
1986	3.47	4.24	3.93	2.72
1987	3.74	4.45	4.24	2.90

a: the calculation is based on elasticities estimated by CD-6. In the calculation, elasticities α and β are normalized as α' and β' such that $\alpha' + \beta' = 1$.

According to this hypothesis, we should observe the following phenomena: (i) while the level of the total factor productivity in the TVE sector increases, the growth rate of the TFP decreases over time; (ii) in regions with a higher level of TFP, the TFP growth rate is lower than in regions where the TFP levels are low.

In Table 4, a decreasing growth rate of the TFP can be observed. This is consistent with the low starting stage hypothesis.

To compare regional TFP levels, let us look at Table 10. This table shows the TFP levels in the TVE sector both at the national level and at the regional level. The estimation of the TFP level is based on the elasticities estimated by CD-6.

Table 10 shows that in the suburban region, the TFP level

is the highest in the nation. In 1982, the TFP level in the suburban region was about 80 percent higher than the level in the interior region and about 30 percent higher than the level in the coastal region. However, since the TFP growth rate of TVEs in the suburban region was the lowest, the gap between TVEs in suburban regions and other regions is shrinking. In 1987, although the TFP level in suburban regions was still the highest, it was about 50 percent higher than that of the interior regions and only 5 percent higher than that of the coastal regions.

Table 11. TFP Growth and Share of TFP Growth
in TVE Output Growth

	1983	1984	1985	1986	1987
Growth of TVE Output[a]	23.1	31.9	32.7	16.0	15.5
Suburb Growth Rate of TFP[b]	12.4	11.3	10.3	9.18	8.10
Stand. Er. of TFP Growth[b]	3.98	4.42	4.87	5.31	5.75
Growth Rate of TFP[c]	6.28	6.28	6.28	6.28	6.28
Stand. Er. of TFP Growth[c]	1.19	1.19	1.19	1.19	1.19
Growth of TVE Output[a]	20.1	26.2	44.8	15.9	25.9
Coast Growth Rate of TFP[b]	17.1	16.0	15.0	13.9	12.8
Stand. Er. of TFP Growth[b]	3.20	3.64	4.08	4.53	5.41
Growth Rate of TFP[c]	11.0	11.0	11.0	11.0	11.0
Stand. Er. of TFP Growth[c]	1.27	1.27	1.27	1.27	1.27
Growth of TVE Output[a]	14.8	32.9	23.8	12.6	19.7
Interior Growth Rate of TFP[b]	13.8	12.7	11.7	10.6	9.52
Stand. Er. of TFP Growth[b]	3.14	3.58	4.02	4.47	5.35
Growth Rate of TFP[c]	7.57	7.57	7.57	7.57	7.57
Stand. Er. of TFP Growth[c]	0.84	0.84	0.84	0.84	0.84

Sources: a: SSB, 1983-1988, at 1980 constant price level;
b: estimated in CD-6;
c: estimated in CD-8.

Table 11 compares the TFP growth rates of TVEs in the three regions. Consistent with the findings in Table 10, according to estimates of both CD-6 and CD-8, the TFP growth rate in the suburban regions is the lowest, and the growth rate in the coastal regions is the highest.

The finding that the region with the highest initial TFP level has the lowest TFP growth rate, and the region with the lowest initial TFP level has a higher TFP growth rate consistent with the low starting stage hypothesis. However, the finding that TVEs in the coastal regions have the highest TFP growth rate but not the lowest initial TFP level cannot easily be explained by the low starting stage hypothesis. This finding may be explained by the open door policy: the TVEs in the coastal regions have more connections with foreign firms; thus, the source of technology transfer is not limited to the state sector.

CONCLUSIONS

This paper investigates the pattern of productivity growth and employment behavior of Chinese rural industry both at the national level and at the provincial level during 1982-1987. The major conclusions of the paper are the following:

(i) A Cobb-Douglas production function provides the best description of the growth of TVEs in the period 1982-1987 among the dozen potential specifications which are tested. The growth rates of the TFP in this function are different across regions, and are decreasing over time. Output elasticities with respect to capital and labor inputs are constant over time and are the same across regions.

(ii) Increases in productivity are an important factor in the extraordinary growth of TVEs. The share of the TFP growth accounts for almost half of the growth of TVE output.[50] This pattern of growth is similar to the growth pattern in Japan and South Korea in the 1960s and the early 1970s. The TFP growth rate of TVEs is much higher than that of Chinese state-owned enterprises and of the USSR state-owned enterprises. These statistical findings contribute to the debate on the efficiency of TVEs and the efficiency comparison between the TVE sector and the state sector.

(iii) The TVEs in the regions with the highest TFP level have the lowest TFP growth rate in the nation. And the TVEs in the regions with the lower TFP levels have the higher TFP growth rate. Meanwhile, the TFP growth rate of TVEs is decreasing over time for all regions. If this growth pattern continues, it is possible that eventually the TFP growth in the TVE sector will be similar to that of the state sector.

With respect to the behavior of TVEs, conflicting evidence has been collected from field research conducted by the World Bank-Chinese Academy of Social Sciences, and Chinese Development Institute etc.: in some areas, the government controls TVEs tightly (e.g. in Wuxi and Shangrao counties[51]); in other localities, TVEs seem to be free enterprises (e.g. in Jieshou and Nanhai counties[52]). Statistical evidence presented in this chapter show that, in general, government involvement in TVEs is strong.

(iv) Evidence of inefficient resource allocation in the TVE sector is discovered: TVE wages are much lower than the marginal product of labor, and the gap between wages and the marginal product is becoming larger; this gap reveals a possible labor shortage in the TVE sector.

(v) Statistical evidence shows that the inefficient resource allocation in the TVE sector may be primarily caused by government involvement in the TVEs; TVEs are forced to adopt (directly or indirectly) wage standards set by the government.

APPENDIX A

To test the hypotheses on the growth of the TFP, on output elasticities, and on substitution elasticity, the following restricted versions of the production functions are estimated and tested step by step according to a 5 percent statistical significance level for the estimates to be acceptable. Restricting α and β to be the same for all regions, allowing α' and β' to vary for different regions, the following CD-2 is obtained.

$$\ln Y_{it} = \bar{a}D + (\bar{\lambda}_1 + \bar{\lambda}_2 t)Dt + (\alpha + \bar{\alpha}'t)D \ln L_{it} +$$

$$(\beta + \bar{\beta}'t))D \ln K_{it} + \varepsilon_{it} \qquad \text{(CD-2)}$$

Restricting the production function further such that in all regions, λ_1 are the same, λ_2 different, the following CD-3 is obtained.

$$\ln Y_{it} = \bar{a}D + (\lambda_1 + \bar{\lambda}_2 t)Dt + (\alpha + \bar{\alpha}'t)D \ln L_{it} +$$

$$(\beta + \bar{\beta}'t))D \ln K_{it} + \varepsilon_{it} \qquad \text{(CD-3)}$$

CD-4 allows and λ_1 and λ_2 to be different in different regions, but restricts α, α', β and β' to be the same in all regions.

$$\ln Y_{it} = \bar{a}D + (\bar{\lambda}_1 + \bar{\lambda}_2 t)Dt + (\alpha + \bar{\alpha}'t)D \ln L_{it} +$$

$$(\beta + \bar{\beta}'t))D \ln K_{it} + \varepsilon_{it} \qquad \text{(CD-4)}$$

Based on CD-4, CD-5 further restricts λ_2 to be the same in all regions.

$$\ln Y_{it} = \overline{a}D + (\overline{\lambda}_1 + \overline{\lambda}_2 t)Dt + (\alpha + \overline{\alpha}'t)D \ln L_{it} +$$

$$(\beta + \overline{\beta}'t)) \ln K_{it} + \varepsilon_{it} \qquad (CD\text{-}5)$$

Restricting elasticities of input factors to be constant over time, CD-5 is simplified to CD-6.

$$\ln Y_{it} = \overline{a}D + (\overline{\lambda}_1 + \overline{\lambda}_2 t)Dt + (\alpha + \overline{\alpha}'t)D \ln L_{it} +$$

$$\beta \ln K_{it} + \varepsilon_{it} \qquad (CD\text{-}6)$$

Relaxing the constraint that substitution elasticity equals to one, CD-6 can be generalized to the following CES-2.

$$\ln Y_{it} = \overline{a}D + (\overline{\lambda}_1 + \lambda_2 t)Dt + v\delta \ln L_{it} + v(1-\delta)D \ln L_{it} -$$

$$0.5pv\delta(1-\delta)(\ln(K_{it}/L_{it}))^2 + \varepsilon_{it} \qquad (CES2)$$

Restricting CD-6 such that in all regions the TFPs are the same, the specification is the following:

$$\ln Y_{it} = \overline{a}D + (\lambda_1 + \lambda_2 t)t + \alpha \ln L_{it} +$$

$$\beta \ln L_{it} + \varepsilon_{it} \qquad (CD\text{-}7)$$

Restricting CD-6 in another way such that the growth rate of the TFP is constant over time, CD-8 is obtained.

$$\ln Y_{it} = \overline{a}D + \overline{\lambda}_1 Dt + \alpha \ln L_{it} + \beta \ln L_{it} + \varepsilon_{it} \qquad (CD\text{-}8)$$

CD-9 forces the TFP growth rate in different regions to be the same and also forces the TFP growth rate to be constant over time.

$$\ln Y_{it} = \overline{a}D + \lambda_1 Dt + \alpha \ln L_{it} + \beta \ln L_{it} + \varepsilon_{it} \qquad \text{(CD-9)}$$

The data used in estimating the production functions are shown in   Table A1. All the data are from SSB, *Statistical Yearbook of China, 1983-1988* and are from He Kang et al. (eds.), *Chinese Agriculture Yearbook 1980-1986.* In the table, Y, K, and L stand for output, capital, and labor respectively, and Numb. stands for the number of TVEs. Output and capital are in billion yuan and are deflated to 1980 prices. Labor is in millions and the number of TVEs is in thousands. The following Table A2 shows the marginal product of labor of TVEs, TVE wages (Wtve), hypothetical TVE worker incomes (Itve), urban collectively-owned enterprise wages (Wcoe), state-owned enterprise wages (Wsoe), and rural laborers' incomes (Wag). The marginal product of labor is estimated based on production function CD-6. Itve is calculated based on the discussion in Section 3(2). All other data   are   from   SSB, *Statistical Yearbook of China, 1983-1988* and are from He Kang et al. (eds.), *Chinese Agriculture Yearbook 1980-1986.*

ENDNOTES

1. This was the policy of the central government under Zhao Ziyang's regime. The above mentioned view are typical views of Zhao's economic advisors. Soon after Zhao's loss of power in June 1989, these views were openly criticized.

2. Many Chinese economists and policy analysts hold this view. Some essays in Byrd and Lin (1990) also reflect this view (e.g. Chapter 3 by Du).

3. The field research and survey problem are the following: (i) the surveys were conducted either only in a few localities (the World Bank-Chinese Academy of Social Sciences project covered four counties -- in China there are more than two thousand counties), or the samples are biased (the Chinese Development Institute project surveyed only the largest TVEs in nine provincial regions -- in China there are 29 provincial regions). Therefore, the results may be too limited or biased to reveal nation-wide trends; (ii) many of the surveys are opinion surveys, the results of which may be biased. In a society based on ideological control and propaganda, when answering questionnaires, subjects may alter their responses to conform to the official ideology rather than expressing their true opinions.

4. Svejnar, J., "Productive Efficiency and Employment," in Byrd and Lin (1990).

5. Because of data limitations, in this paper "suburban region" is defined as suburbs of Beijing, Tianjin, and Shanghai.

6. Wang, Tuoyu, "Regional Imbalance," in Byrd and Lin (1990).

7. By assuming that all profits are distributed to the workers of TVEs, hypothetical worker incomes are equal to wage plus per worker profit.

8. Ma Hong, Sun Shangqing, *Zhongguo Jingji Jiegou Wenti Yanjiu (Research on the Problems of Economic Structure in China)*, Beijing: People's Press, 1981.

9. Ma Hong (ed.), *Xiandai Zhongguo Jingji Shidian (Mini Encyclopedia of Modern Chinese Economy)*, Beijing: CASS Press, 1982, p.213.

10. This policy or campaign emphasized self-reliance and the complete elimination of markets.

11. This policy emphasized the simultaneous growth of modern and traditional industry, and the simultaneous growth of central and local government-controlled industry.

12. Hereafter, urban collectively-owned enterprises mainly refer to COEs in counties. According to the official statistical definition, counties are urban areas.

13. Wong, C., (1989), "Maoism and Development: A Reconsideration of Local Self-reliance in Financing Rural Industrialization," in Wong, C. et al. (eds.).

14. *Zhongguo nongye nianjian (Chinese Agricultural Yearbook), 1986*, p.321.

15. *Zhongguo nongyie nianjian (Chinese Agricultural Yearbook), 1980*. As formal policy, these regulations are considered a milestone for the growth of TVEs, and the growth of TVEs accelerated. However, as mentioned above, the real

change began in the mid-1970s when the central government relaxed its control.

16. *Statistical Yearbook of China, 1988,* pp. 292-294. The statistics quoted here and in the next paragraph include also those of privately-owned enterprises.

17. *Nongye Nianjian, 1986.*

18. *Renmin Ribao (haiwai ban) (People's Daily, Oversees edition),* Feb. 28, 1989.

19. *Statistical Yearbook of China, 1988,* pp.292-294.

20. The official statistics for gross national industrial production (GNIP) do not include production of private enterprises. Therefore we calculate GNIP* in the following way: GNIP* = GNIP + (GTVPIP - GTVIP) = 1182.9 + (324.3 - 244.7) = 1262.5 billion yuan. Here, GNIP is the official figure for GNIP; GTVPIP denotes gross TVP industrial production and GTVIP denotes gross TV industrial production. In these calculations, the source of the data is *Statistical Yearbook of China, 1988.*

21. In this paper, "local governments" refer to township and village governments.

22. *Zhongguo nongye nianjian (Chinese Agricultural Yearbook),* 1980. Translated by the author.

23. "National Academic Conference on TVEs, 1984." *Zhongguo nongye nianjian, 1985.*

24. Rural Policy Research Division of the Central Committee Secretariat, Center for Rural Development of the State Council, "A Summary of the Nationwide Rural Socio-economic Sampling Survey," *Zhongguo Nongye Nianjian*

(Chinese Agricultural Yearbook), 1986.

In a sample survey, researchers found that 77.5 percent of the village administrative budgets came from the VE. Administrators of sample villages stated that one of the major motivations for setting up VEs was to expand their administrative budgets. The survey was reported in Li Yandong, "Cunban qiye de yunxing jizhi yu xiangzhen qiye de fazhan -- 1986 nian nongcun guding guanchadian zhuanti fenxi (The operation mechanism of VEs and the growth of TVEs -- an analysis of the results of the 1986 rural area sampling survey), " Unpublished paper, 1987.

25. World Bank field research finds that in Wuxi county, 78.9% of the TE sample obtained raw materials at prices lower than those in the market through the township government, while only 5.3% of the PEs did; in the Jieshou county's sample, low-priced raw materials were only distributed among TEs. With respect to investment or capital supply, in Wuxi county, 21.1% of total capital of TEs was allocated through the township governments, while other enterprises received none. In Jieshou county, a similar situation was reported. Owned and protected by the township government, TEs enjoy a higher status in the eyes of industrial and commercial administration bureaus, and tax and supply departments than enterprises under other ownership arrangements. The findings were reported in Song Lina, Du He, "The Role of Township Governments in Rural Industrialization," in Byrd and Lin (eds.) (1990).

26. Song Lina, "Convergence: A Comparison of Township-run Firms and Local State Enterprises," in Byrd and Lin (eds.), (1990).

27. Official retail price indexes are constructed in such a way that the indexes reflect official prices, negotiation prices, and market prices for consumer goods and agricultural producer goods. The largest portion of TVE products are consumer

goods and agricultural producer goods. By Chinese official conventions, TVEs are a sub-sector of the agricultural sector, and thus many capital goods used by TVEs can be classified as agricultural producer goods. For these reasons, the best proxy for a price index is the retail price index.

28. State Statistical Bureau, *Statistical Yearbook of China, 1983-1988. Agricultural Yearbook of China, 1983-1987.*

29. By adjusting fixed asset data, Chen K., et al., (1988) were able to get significant non zero TFP estimates for Chinese state-owned industry from 1950 to 1985. However, their way of adjusting input factors is problematic. I will discuss this issue later in the paper.

30. Regions are grouped according to their similarities in levels of development. The most "developed" region is the suburbs of the major cities. Since except the data from Beijing, Tianjin, and Shanghai, there are no data available for other major suburbs, in this paper "suburban region" refers to the suburbs of the three largest cities. The second most developed area is the coastal region, which includes Heilongjiang, Jilin, Liaoning, Shandong, Jiangsu, Zhejiang, Fujian, Guangdong. The underdeveloped region is the interior region, which includes all other provinces.

31. Kmenta, J., (1967), "On Estimation of CES Production Function," *International Economic Review*, 8: 1880-89.

32. According to the official statistics, TVEs pay wages to workers and earn profits. The profits are distributed to collective welfare funds and for capital formation. If TVEs are labor-managed firms, the method of distributing profits should be completely determined by the workers collectively. Thus profits can be regarded as part of the workers' income, and workers voluntarily spend this part of

their income in the way reported.

33. The same result appears when the communities which run the TVEs have complete autonomy; that is the people in the communities make their decisions collectively. However, in this situation, TVEs still do not have autonomy, and the autonomy of the communities can be regarded as the autonomy of the local governments.

34. From $Itve_{it} = Wtve_{it} + \pi_{it}/L_{it} = MPL_{it}$, one gets

$Wtve_{it} = MPL_{it} - \pi_{it}/L_{it}$.

35. Some evidence was collected that the government does force the TVEs to adopt the SOE wage standards. This will be discussed later.

36. A possible rationale for government restrictions on TVE employment is to guarantee a given agricultural labor force, and thus maintain food production. Chen Yun, the only senior Party leader who can compete with Deng Xiaoping, especially on economic issues, gives food production a very high priority.

37. Similar situations occur in Qinghai, Gansu, Xinjiang, and other provinces.

38. Meng Xin, "The Rural Labor Market," in Byrd and Lin (eds.) (1990).

39. Wu Quhui, Wang Hansheng and Xu Xinxin, "Noneconomic Factors Determining Workers' Income," in Byrd and Lin (eds.) (1990).

40. *Jingji Cankao*, Mar.10, 1987.

41. Sun Zizheng, (1989), "Liangshi Shengchan Zhongde Difang Zhengfu Juice Xingwei Paoxi (An Analysis of Local Government Behavior in Decisions for Food Production)," *Jingji Yanjiu*, 1989, No.5.

42. Hou Xiaohong et al. (1988), "Xianjieduan Nongcun Shengyu Laodongli Xingwei Tezheng (Current Behavioral Features of the Rural Surplus Labor Force)," *Jingji Yanjiu*, 1988, No.2.

43. Lin Qingsong, (1987), "Shanxi Yuanpingxian Xiangzhen Qiye Kaocha (An Investigation of TVPs in Yuanping county of Shanxi province)," in Institute of Economics, CASS, *Zhongguo Xiangzhen Qiye de Jingji Fazhan yu Jingji Tizhi (Economic Development and the Economic System of Chinese TVPs)*. Beijing: Chinese Economic Press, 1987.

44. Luo Yousheng et al., (1988), "Tudi Jiating Chengbaozhi de Xianzhuang Panduan yu Biange Gouxiang (The Land Household Contract System: Evaluation of its Current Situation and Some Ideas for Further Reforms)," *Jingji Yanjiu*, 1988, No.11.

45. Lin Qingsong, (1987), "Shanxi Yuanpingxian Xiangzhen Qiye Kaocha (An Investigation of TVPs in Yuanping county of Shanxi province)," in Institute of Economics, CASS, *Zhongguo Xiangzhen Qiye de Jingji Fazhan yu Jingji Tizhi (The Economic Development and the Economic System of Chinese TVPs)*. Beijing: Chinese Economic Press, 1987.

46. The index TFP $= Y/(\alpha L + \beta K)$ is equivalent to the following production function: $Y = TFP(\alpha L + \beta K)$. In general, this linear function is not a proper specification for a production function. For more theoretical criticism of the index, see Domar, E. (1962), "On Total Productivity and All That," *JPE*, 70:597-608; and see Lave, L.B. (1966), *Technological Change: Its Conception and*

Measurement.   Englewood Cliffs, NJ: Prentice-Hall.

47. Their major revision is the subtraction of the "nonproductive capital input" and the "nonproductive labor input" from the total factor inputs. By revising the data in this way, they find a significant positive rate of growth of the TFP in the state sector (e.g. the TFP growth rate estimated directly from the production function based on the original data is 0.5 percent; the estimate based on the revised data is 1.3 percent). However, there are conceptual problems to this method of manipulating the data. In a centrally planned economy like the Chinese state sector, wages have nothing to do with the marginal product of labor and are much lower than the marginal product of labor (according to this study, even in the most market-oriented sector -- the TVE sector -- the correlation between wages and the marginal product of labor is extremely weak and wages are almost three times lower than the marginal product of labor). Urban employees cannot live on their wages without subsidies. In fact, employees of SOEs get subsidized housing, medical care, and other social welfare services, very often directly from the enterprises where they work. A major part of the so-called nonproductive input factors are used for these purposes. These are in fact an essential part of the employees income and thus an essential part of the production costs. Therefore, it is not a proper approach to subtract all the nonproductive input factors to estimate the aggregate production functions.

48. These results are similar to the TFP growth rate of the USSR state sector in the 1960s and the early 1970s: the upper limit is similar to the TFP growth rate of the USSR state sector in 1960-70, and the lower limit is similar to the rate for the USSR state sector in 1970-75.

49. According to the upper limit of the estimation, the share of the TFP growth rate in the total growth rate in the Chinese state sector is lower than that in the USSR in the 1960s and higher than that in the USSR in early the 1970s.

50. This is the result of the "best estimation" -- CD-6. According to the estimate of lower limit of the growth rate, it accounts for one third of the TVE output growth.

51. See Meng Xin, "The Rural Labor Market," and Wu, Q., H. Wang, and X.Xu, "Noneconomic Factors Determining Workers' Income," in Byrd and Lin (eds.), (1990).

52. Ibid.

Chapter 3

Chinese Township Village Enterprises
as
Vaguely Defined Cooperatives[1]

1. INTRODUCTION

Fully one third of the world's population currently seems to be moving away from centrally planned socialism towards some form of a market economy. Suppose we refer to the broad process of making a transition from some form of socialism to some form of capitalism as a process of transformation. It appears as if there are essentially two different models of transformation.

In principle, the more revolutionary changes are required by what might be called the standard model. Basically, the standard model involves making a transition to the standard capitalist economy as quickly as possible, with the essential core of the transition being centered on the aggressive establishment of well defined private property rights. This model is more or less familiar to us because the existence of well-defined private property rights seems an absolutely essential precondition to the proper functioning of a capitalist market economy. Such a basic truth comes at us from theory and from practice. To a western-trained economist, the centrality and immediacy to any transformation process of establishing well-defined private property seems so self evident as to hardly merit discussion. It is little wonder that, leaving aside the sometimes more immediate issues of macroeconomic stabilization, the officially sanctioned position of Western governments and international lending organizations places the highest priority on the rapid establishment of well-defined property rights.

While it seems fair to say that the standard model serves as a general policy guide for East European transformation to a West-European-style economy, this does not mean that the policy has been implemented easily. In fact, one of the major problems with East European transformation has concerned the great difficulty of establishing well defined private property rights. In this sense, a fair statement might be that the problem with the East European experience thus far is not that it has followed the standard model, but rather that it has not followed the standard model sufficiently thoroughly because private property rights have not been instituted in a sufficiently consistent, clear, rapid or thoroughgoing fashion.

The second, more evolutionary model of transformation is perhaps somewhat less familiar. It might be called the Chinese model, because of its close identification with China.[2] This model calls for a more gradualist strategy of allowing market oriented enterprises to develop from within the interstices of the economy. Rather than being transformed dramatically by privatization in the short run, state enterprises, particularly medium and small ones, are pushed, outcompeted, and outgrown by non-state sector firms and are gradually replaced in the long run. The non-state sector in China's rural areas basically means the TVE (Township Village Enterprise).

While it will be important to present the Chinese model in greater detail, and to quantify more precisely the role of TVEs, for present purposes it suffices to note that the TVE is a major driving force in the Chinese reform.[3] The primary point of this paper is to argue that the TVE is essentially what might be called a vaguely defined cooperative. We realize that viewing TVEs as vaguely defined cooperatives is likely to be controversial and develop this argument later in some detail; here only a brief summary is provided.

It is well documented that a typical TVE is not a privately-owned firm.[4] A TVE is basically a communal organization very far removed from having well defined property rights. There is a deep involvement of the community government in its operation. The legal system related to the TVE is also ill-defined from a capitalist perspective. The typical TVE seems almost the exact opposite of the type of private organization at the center of the standard model, as the TVE appears to go almost completely against the grain of standard property rights theory.

Yet the Chinese model, with a central role being played by TVEs as the dominant form of non-state enterprise, is in fact enormously successful, much more successful so far than any actual applications of the standard model. Casual observation and independent econometric studies (Svejnar (1990), Pitt and Putterman (1992)) indicate that TVEs are as efficient as private firms. So we have on our hands a significant paradox. Why do vaguely-defined cooperatives seem to perform so well?   Does this not represent some contradiction with the basic precepts of property rights theory?   Can a transforming country actually choose between the two models, and can a transition strategy be reliably based on the performance of vaguely defined cooperatives?

This brings us to the second, and more speculative, part of the paper. It seems to us that the above questions, and some other important issues about transformation, are difficult to address meaningfully from within the framework that underlies the standard model. In the second part of this paper we attempt to sketch the outlines of a possible expanded framework for addressing these issues.

It seems fair to say that standard property right theory aspires to be a universal or culture-free theory. The theory assumes, explicitly or implicitly, that all people are indiscriminately non-cooperative regardless of their cultural background. Under this assumption, a major role of ownership is to resolve conflicts or to enforce cooperation in an economic organization. However, if there are variations in cooperative behavior among people of different societies, then the significance of ownership in solving conflicts in economic organizations may also vary.

By using a fundamental concept of repeated game theory, it is possible to integrate formally the seemingly cultural element of a cooperative spirit with standard property rights theory to arrive at a somewhat more general version of property rights theory. In this paper we propose, at the level of verbal theorizing, a more general approach. This general approach may reconcile the originally posed paradox, and may have implications for understanding other interesting and puzzling phenomena, such as certain aspects of the Japanese economy.

The paper, then, divides into two parts. The first part, which constitutes the basic message of the paper, argues that TVEs are best viewed as vaguely defined cooperatives with weak or poorly developed property rights. Yet, as we will show, the performance of the TVE's is at least as good as the private firms that they dominate in the non-state sector and much better than the state-owned enterprises. Thus, the outstanding TVE performance would appear to represent a paradox or challenge for traditional property rights theory.

In principle, there might be several ways to answer the challenge. We propose in the second part of the paper one particular way of dealing with the issue, based on a notion of cooperative culture. While this approach seems useful to us, we would not claim that it represents the only way of resolving the problem. In any event, the second part of the paper is necessarily more speculative than the first and should be treated as such.

The rest of the paper is organized as follows. To facilitate the later discussions, section 2 gives a brief survey of standard property rights theory. Then, the standard model of transition is briefly discussed in section 3 and contrasted with the Chinese model. Section 4, constituting the core of the paper, describes, with some evidence, the TVE as a vaguely defined cooperative and shows the basic contradictions with standard property rights theory. In section 5, which begins the more speculative part of the paper, we describe the fundamental folk theorem concept of repeated game theory and show how it may be applied to provide a theoretical foundation for reconciling orthodox property rights theory with a cooperative cultural element. Within this framework of a generalized property rights theory, the central paradox of the paper is seemingly reconciled, although, as we emphasize, this is not the only possible reconciliation. Some further implications of the generalized property rights approach are discussed in section 6.

2. THE STANDARD PROPERTY RIGHTS THEORY

Our basic thesis is that the Chinese township-village enterprises are best described as vaguely defined cooperatives that perform extremely well in practice despite seeming not to be based on well defined private property rights in the standard or conventional sense. To develop further our thesis, we need to state the essence of the standard or conventional property rights theory.

There is no single universally accepted statement of so-called property rights theory. Most presentations of the theory are essentially verbal expositions representing a combination of philosophical thinking, empirical generalizations, and reasoned theoretical assertions.[5] There are a few rigorously constructed theoretical models; these theories are developed under more or less the same culture free assumptions as the verbal formulations.[6] Despite the lack of a single canonical form that can readily be cited, it seems fair to say that there is a consistent spirit to the basic thesis of the property rights school. Its essence may be summarized as follows.

In property rights theory, the existence of well-defined private property rights is viewed as a basic precondition to the proper functioning of a capitalist market economy.[7] Well defined property rights typically includes the following three basic elements:

(1) To every property is assigned a well defined owner or owners with exclusive rights of ownership.

(2) To the owner of the property goes the residual income accruing to the assets.

(3) The owner has the right to control or determine use of the existing assets, to restructure the property, and to sell or lease it.[8]

Concerning applications of the property rights approach to the firm, the theory identifies the owner of the firm with the ultimate director of its important decisions. The theory implies, and this is a fourth point, that

(4) Without well defined private ownership the firm will tend to operate relatively badly, and any system without widespread well defined property rights will tend to perform relatively badly.[9]

There may be many reasons for this fourth point. One reason frequently cited in the comparative systems and the transition economics literature is that without true private ownership there tend to arise problems associated with the soft budget syndrome; since there are no clearly identified owners to pay for mistakes or bad luck, someone else pays, typically the state.[10] When true property owners or residual claimants exist, it is ultimately they who are uniquely positioned, by having the proper rights and the incentives, to: observe or to monitor input behavior, to negotiate and to enforce contracts on behalf of the firm, to hire and lay off or fire workers, to sell off or buy property, and to take other decisions to increase the profitability of the firm because it is they who ultimately must pay for mistakes or bad luck. When private owners cannot readily obtain compensation for losses from the state, then all of the rights enjoyed by the owner play a critical role in blocking the infinite regress of inefficiency and shirking that typically characterizes the soft budget syndrome of a system without true ownership of private property. While this section relates an extremely succinct version of the property rights approach, which glosses over some fine points, we believe the four features highlighted here fairly summarize the essence of the theory.

3. THE STANDARD MODEL AND
THE CHINESE MODEL

In describing the standard model of transition, we will concentrate on principles or fundamental strategies rather than the actuality of implementation. Our discussion will be very brief because the basic features are familiar.[11] Remember that we are operating at a high level of abstraction, glossing over many possible differences among many different countries.

A common strand of the standard model is the central role of private property within an appropriate monetary and fiscal structure. Transition strategy is centered on developing the basic institutions of capitalism. These include well-defined ownership rights in the conventional sense, with a corresponding legal system, commercial code, contract and bankruptcy laws, and so forth. A reward system that makes the owner the true residual claimant is viewed as critical to prevent shirking throughout the system. The wedge of true private property blocks the infinite regress of inefficiency and shirking that characterized the old socialist regime, because the true property owners have the power, and incentives, to harden budget constraints, stop losses, and encourage profitability at the point where the owners are wedged into the hierarchy.

The standard model focuses sharply on privatizing formerly state-owned enterprises. There are, as we know, various strategies of privatization, but the underlying goal is always to introduce well defined private property rights in a context of market competition.[12] Any compromise with tainted institutions like producer cooperatives, worker management, state-private partnerships, semi-private or semi-cooperative firms, and so forth, is viewed with hostility. The weak property rights and loose reward structures associated with such ill-defined institutions are deemed likely to result in the same poor performance, for many of the same reasons, from which the formerly socialist economies are trying to escape.

As a guide to policy, the standard model follows well the precepts of contemporary economic theory, most especially the tenets of the property rights school. Of course, it is one thing to have a guide to policy and quite another thing to enact the policy. It seems fair to say that there have been varying degrees of success in establishing property rights in Eastern Europe, but nowhere has it been easy or routine. In other words, the existence of what we are calling the standard model does not mean that the model has been quickly or easily implemented. In fact, the opposite has more nearly been the case for Eastern Europe.

The Chinese model, in contrast to the standard model, was not consciously designed as a transformation strategy at the beginning of the reforms, but evolved as the reforms progressed. Its essence is that new non-state enterprises, of which the TVE is the overwhelmingly predominant form, will outcompete and outgrow the state enterprises and thereby replace them gradually.

The township-village enterprise (TVE) thus plays a pivotal role in the Chinese model, and it is to this organization that we now turn in the next, central, section of the paper. We are aware that the phenomena under examination are extremely complex and multifaceted, but in this paper we have attempted to step back and paint a broad brush picture that is true in spirit, even while exceptions can be argued for some details. While the actual situation may be very complicated when viewed close up, it is possible to summarize fairly the basic features of the TVE at a high level of generalization. We will put some important qualifications into footnotes.

4. THE TVE AS A VAGUELY DEFINED COOPERATIVE

What is a TVE?

According to the official definition, TVEs are collectively-owned enterprises located in townships or villages.[13] More specifically, all the residents in the township or village that establishes the TVE own the firm collectively. The property rights of TVEs can only be executed collectively through the representatives of the community. In practice, the most common case is that a community government is regarded as the representative of the residents, and thus it is the *de facto* executive owner of the TVEs in the community.

Concerning the management of TVEs, it is typical that the control rights are partly delegated to managers through a contract, officially called the management responsibility contract. In a typical case, employees of a TVE collectively sign a contract with the executive owner, the community government.[14] Then the manager of the TVE is determined jointly by the community government and the employees. Thus, the manager is a representative of the employees and of the government. The degree of the community government's role in the appointment of TVE managers varies from case to case, but it is rarely negligible.[15]

TVE Performance

Table 1 summarizes some relevant growth rates for the period 1979 to 1991. Y is output, K is capital, and L is labor. SOE stands for state owned industrial enterprises, while TVE stands for township village enterprises. These two categories are not strictly comparable. Data limitations prevent separating collectively-owned TVEs from privately-owned rural enterprises. The category covered under TVE in Table 1 is somewhat broader than TVEs proper because it includes all rural non-state enterprises. Because the output of TVEs proper constitutes about three fourths of the output of rural non-state enterprises, and studies have shown TVE productivity performance to be no lower than that of comparable private firms (Svejnar (1990), Pitt and Putterman (1992)), for the purposes of this paper it seems permissible to identify TVEs with rural non-state enterprises. Data limitations likewise prevent the separation of industrial from non-industrial activities within the TVE sector; but industry is approximately 75 percent of TVE output, and since it is widely held to be the most efficient TVE activity, we may regard the TVE productivity growth rates shown in Table 1 as reasonable lower bound estimates of TVE industry.[16] For purposes of comparison, output growth rates for aggregate national industrial output are also included in Table 1.

TABLE 1
COMPARISON OF GROWTH AND EFFICIENCY IN THE STATE AND
TVE SECTORS 1979-1991

	Nat'l Indus	SOE Industry	TVE
Output	13.3	8.4	25.3
Capital	-	7.8	16.5
Labor	-	3.0	11.9
TFP growth	-	4.0	12.0

Source: Official series on gross value of output, net value of fixed assets, and total employment for SOE Industry and TVE sector; output and capital deflated by ratio of official SOE gross industrial output (at current prices) to official SOE industrial output index (at comparable prices). All data from State Statistical Bureau Yearbooks, 1986-1992. Growth rates shown are annual percentages averaged over the period. An appendix with detailed calculations and explanations is available from the authors upon request.

Before discussing total factor productivity (TFP)calculations, a word of caution is in order. Primarily for technical reasons about the appropriate deflation procedure, but also more generally because there are alternative ways of treating the data, a precise calculation of TFP may involve some controversy. We present here our best estimates, but investigating and explaining TFP calculations is not the central topic of this paper. The main point we would emphasize is that the estimates we present are sufficiently robust to support easily the basic conclusions we draw.

Total factor productivity is calculated as a residual after subtracting from output growth a weighted average of the growth rates of labor and capital inputs. The weights we use are .7 for labor and .3 for capital, corresponding crudely to a rough worldwide consensus that labor's share of income is somewhere between 2/3 and 3/4.

Table 1 reveals several important insights. Total factor productivity grows approximately three times faster for TVEs than for the corresponding SOEs. With TFP growth averaging 12% annually, TVEs are expanding primarily by intensive technological progress and only secondarily by extensively siphoning off inputs from other potential users.

It is beyond the scope of this paper to provide an exhaustive survey of the literature on comparative efficiency of Chinese SOEs and TVEs. Here it must suffice to state that results of several research papers, some drawn from quite different data sources, are consistent with the basic contention that TFP growth, as defined here, is much higher for TVEs than for SOEs.[17]

The TVE growth performance shown in Table 1 is so outstanding by world historical standards that it does not seem unwarranted to label it spectacular. The difference between the growth rate of aggregate national industrial output and the growth rate of SOE industry is almost five full percentage points. Since the spectacular TVE growth rate of 25% per year is largely accounting for this difference, it should not be an exaggeration to identify the TVE sector as a major engine, perhaps the major engine, of recent Chinese economic growth.

As a result of the extraordinarily rapid growth of TVEs, in little more than a decade the status of the TVE sector has changed from that of a subsidiary sub-sector of agriculture to the second largest sector in the national economy.[18] Compared with the private sector, the TVE is the dominant form. In 1991, 74 percent of total industrial output produced in rural areas was from cooperatives, which includes 67 percent from TVEs and 7 percent from producer cooperatives, while the private sector accounted for 26 percent.

The high efficiency and rapid growth of the TVE sector has exerted deep influences on the state sector in two major aspects. First, the competition has forced state enterprises to work very hard to avoid making losses.[19] Second, instead of being replaced by massive privatization, as in most East European strategies, if not in practice, the relative role of state enterprises has been gradually reduced as they are outcompeted and outgrown by the TVEs. According to an official prediction by the Chinese State Statistical Bureau, in the year 2,000 a full half of industrial output will be produced by collectively-owned enterprises, in which the TVE sector is the dominant part; the state sector and private sector will each produce one quarter (*China Daily*, July 15, 1992).

The TVE as a Vaguely Defined Cooperative

To rationalize the success of the TVEs, many Western economists have regarded them as actually being private firms under the protective label of a collective enterprise. But this is not true in general, even though some counter examples can always be found. While we will explain this theme presently, we note here that it is already well documented in the literature that a typical TVE is not a privately-owned firm (Lin (1987), Byrd and Lin (1990), Oi (1992), Nee (1992)).

There is another argument: because of political reasons TVEs are restricted from becoming true capitalist firms based on well defined private property rights. Although this argument may, perhaps, provide a plausible explanation for the existence of the TVE form, it cannot explain the seemingly extraordinary success of their organizational form. Actually, the fact that TVEs are so successful would appear to contradict the main tenets of property rights theory.[20]

If TVEs must be forced into a traditional classification, then they are more like producer cooperatives then anything else.[21] But we prefer to use the term vaguely defined cooperatives to label the collectively owned TVEs, because TVEs seems to be especially ill-defined even by the standards of traditional producer cooperatives.

The following features of the TVE as a vaguely defined cooperative seem especially contradictory with the traditional four basic tenets of property rights theory previously noted:

(1) For the typical TVE there is no owner in the spirit of traditional property rights theory. Nominally, TVEs are collectively-owned enterprises, meaning all the community members are nominal owners. In a typical case, these collective owners do not have clearly defined shares as the term is normally understood. Indeed, there are no shares, formally speaking.

Consistent with this fact, there do not exist any such terms as share holders or even owners to describe this aspect of community membership. Actually, there is no commonly used Chinese word for such a person, neither in common parlance nor in legal documents. The closest Chinese term is *cun-min*, meaning resident of the village. We will use the word resident throughout this paper to emphasize the discrepancy with standard property rights precepts.

In a typical case, participation in a TVE is not a decision made by the residents voluntarily and independently.[22] Instead, their participation is determined by their residency and mandated by the community government, through such actions as assigning households to donate money to a TVE (*lingdao tanpai*) or requiring personal investment as a precondition for being hired by the TVE (*yizi dailao*) (Deng (1992)).[23]

The community government is the *de facto* executive owner of the TVEs. Many Chinese economists report that TVEs are usually controlled by local governments and typically there is no separation between the communal government and the TVEs. These reports describe a situation where many TVEs do not have genuine autonomy in business transactions; the communal government has major influence in the determination of managerial personnel and employment.[24] A field research report reads: "it is very common to see that the basic rights (of TVEs) are in the hands of the Party and (communal) government apparatus, i.e. TVEs are not genuine cooperative enterprises. A significant portion of the net profit (of TVEs) is used for the administrative budget of TV governments."[25]

In summary, none of the residents or the executive owner have the exclusive rights of ownership associated with traditional property rights theory. Moreover, there are legal restrictions to prevent a TVE from converting to a *de facto* privately-owned firm. For example, in the case where a TVE is contracted out to a manager or an individual, the law requires that "all the assets (including the incremental part contributed by the contractor) are still owned by all the labor mass collectively."[26]   That is, the individual contractor is formally prevented from owning the TVE.

(2) There is no residual claimant in the traditional sense. The typical resident waits passively to receive or to enjoy the benefits, of which the major part is not in monetary form but in the form of communal social investment, which is shared by everyone in the community. The amount of the benefit and the form of the benefit which the resident can get are determined by the community government and the manager of the firm.

The residents or the executive owner of a TVE do not have the full right to consume or to dispose of the after-tax income that they have in principle earned from the TVE. In fact, about sixty percent or more of the after-tax profits of TVEs cannot legally be distributed directly to the residents, but must be reserved for the TVEs. Most of this reserve fund is reinvested, with the remainder used as a collective welfare fund and a bonus fund within the firm.[27] Even for the income distributed to the residents, which accounts for less than forty percent of the after-tax profits, the residents still do not have the full rights of disposing with it as they please, since it is intended for social purposes.[28]

Although most workers of a typical TVE are among the residents of the township or village, their wages are out of their control, even collectively. For example, field researches found that some community governments, e.g., in Shangrao county, force TVEs to copy or to adopt the wage system of the state firms in that county (Meng (1990)); in some other areas, e.g. in

Wu Xi county, the total wage bills of TVEs must be approved by community government (Wu, Wang and Xu (1990)). Consistent with these field research results, two econometric studies find that the wages of TVEs are lower than their marginal labor productivities, lower than wages of state enterprises, and are not correlated with the profitability of the TVEs (Xu (1994), Pitt and Putterman (1992)).

(3) In a typical case, the TVE assets are non-sellable, non-transferable, and non-heritable both for the residents and for the executive owner. Residents of the township or village will automatically lose their nominal residency if they leave the community, while an outside individual will automatically gain residency by marriage to a resident of the township/village.[29] Furthermore, the residents of TVEs do not have the right to determine the use of the existing assets. Residents do not have any individual control rights, although they may have some influence on the operation of the TVE collectively.[30]

As for the executive owner of a TVE, the community government, not being a legal owner, does not have the residual right of control over a TVE either. For example, in a typical case the government is restrained from firing workers who are residents of the township/village where the TVE is located. Moreover, there are several other formal legal requirements and restrictions on the roles of the local government as executive owner.[31] Not only is the community government's role different from a private owner, but also its right of control over a TVE is more restrictive than the state government's role *vis-a-vis* state firms in the sense that community governments have to take into account in their decision making the preferences of residents. Field research has found that decisions on the establishment of new TVEs were often discussed and made collectively at village meetings (Byrd (1990).

In recent years, some joint stock township-village companies (JSTVCs) that nominally issue shares have appeared. While there is no telling what the future holds, for the time being such firms are still only a tiny fraction of TVEs, except for a few townships. Even in Guangdong province, which is regarded as one of the most advanced provinces in promoting a joint stock company system, JSTVCs accounted for less than 8 percent of TVEs.[32] Furthermore, rather than representing a clear movement towards privatization, as some people imagined, such firms usually operate within a collective structure in the sense that the bulk of shares is held collectively. In a typical case, after converting to a joint stock company, 80 percent of the shares of a TVE would be held collectively through the company or the township-village government, while 20% of shares are sold to the individual employees of the firm. And the stock held by an individual is non-sellable, non-transferable, often even non-heritable.[33]

A vivid example that is documented concerns the Zhoucun district of Zibo city in Shandong province, one of the model regions most celebrated for advancing JSTVCs. In 1992, of total stock shares of more than 800 JSTVCs in that district, some 94 percent were held collectively, while only 6 percent were privately owned (ZZERO (1992), pp. 45-46).

(4) Even without well defined ownership, the TVEs still operate efficiently. This anomaly has also been noticed by other economists. "Entrepreneurial performance in the TVP sector has been especially remarkable in an environment in which ownership and property rights with respect to industrial assets are not clear and pure private ownership is rare in the smallest concerns." (Byrd (1990), p.189).

According to property rights theory, TVEs should be operating less efficiently than true private firms. Yet, the facts seem otherwise. An econometric study based on panel data of more than 400 TVEs and private firms in 4 counties over 16 years shows that "private ownership and community ownership appear to have similar effects on productivity" (Svejnar (1990), p.253). In the regression, ownership dummy variables are used to investigate vaguely defined cooperatives such as village enterprises and clearly defined cooperatives and private firms such as joint household, family and individual firms, or joint venture firms. The result of the regression shows that the difference between the coefficients of the different ownership dummy variables is statistically insignificant. In a more recent econometric study investigating 200 TVEs and private rural firms distributed in 10 provinces with annual observations from 1984 to 1989, Pitt and Putterman (1992) obtained a very similar result. These studies suggest that productivity in TVEs is similar to private firms, or at least that ownership does not matter in the sample investigated.

Consistent with their good performance, TVEs are subject to hard budget constraints. As evidence of the hard budget constraint on the TVEs, in 1989 about one sixth, or three million, township-village enterprises went bankrupt, or were taken over by other TVEs, while almost all loss-making state-owned enterprises were bailed out by the state.[34] As a result of hard budget constraints, in 1990-91 the loss-making township and village enterprises accounted for about 6 percent of all TVEs. By contrast, more than half of state enterprises were loss-making.[35]

The Basic Paradox

According to almost any version of standard mainstream property rights theory, what we are calling the Chinese model should represent a recipe for economic disaster. Without a true owner who has the clear rights and incentives to operate the firm for maximum profits, there ought to be inefficiency and shirking in TVEs. As a result, the TVEs should operate relatively badly. A transformation strategy centered on vaguely-defined cooperatives, even with a hard budget constraint, would seem like the farthest thing imaginable from conventional wisdom in this area.

The central paradox is the enormous success of the Chinese model in practice, contrasted with the predictions of the standard theory and also with the sputtering, tentative, comparatively less successful experience of the standard model. Why do theory and practice seem so diametrically opposed in this important area? Of course, one could attempt to argue that the standard model was never really tried in Eastern Europe or elsewhere. But this explanation begs many further questions and still leaves a big gap between theory and practice in explaining the success of the Chinese experience.

5. COOPERATIVE CULTURE: A POSSIBLE RECONCILIATION OF THE PARADOX

Why do China's vaguely defined cooperative TVEs perform so well? In keeping with the necessarily compressed nature of this paper, there is not space here to explore fully all the possible explanations. Several factors may play a role. We would like to emphasize in this paper one line of thought that seems to us particularly appropriate, even if it should be regarded as somewhat speculative at this stage because other explanations are logically possible.

Conventional property rights theory may be inadequate here because it is missing a critical dimension. The key missing element is the ability of a group to solve potential conflicts internally, without explicit rules, laws, rights, procedures and so forth. To make this idea more operational, and more internally consistent, we consider a theoretical framework.[36] It is possible to criticize this theoretical framework as, in the end, doing little more than elaborating the syllogism that China's vaguely defined cooperative enterprises perform outstandingly well because China's culture is unique and different. Yet we feel it is useful to go more deeply into the structure of a general argument that might reconcile the paradox, both for its own sake and because this line of reasoning could bear on many issues in economics other than the one being addressed here.

A word about methodology may be in order. In this second part of the paper we are largely trying to synthesize and apply already known theoretical results to an important issue not adequately treated so far in the literature. Thus, the treatment here is largely at the level of verbal theorizing, although we believe that a rigorous formulation will ultimately be possible, but difficult. Also, in trying to state our case succinctly, some simplifications and generalizations are inevitable.

The Folk Theorem of Repeated Games and Cooperative Culture

Let us consider the prisoner's dilemma non-cooperative game.[37] The only solution to the one-shot prisoner's dilemma game is the selfish Nash equilibrium, which is Pareto inferior to the cooperative solution. However, when the prisoner's dilemma game is played repeatedly, a much richer set of results is possible. Actually, a continuum of solutions is possible, which can often be Pareto ranked, corresponding to a greater or lesser degree of 'as if' cooperation. Thus, there is a sense in which a non-cooperative repeated game can yield the kinds of outcomes typically associated with cooperation, collusion, or binding agreements. This family of results is so important, and it has been known for so long, that it has been given a name: the so-called Folk Theorem of game theory.

The Folk Theorem states that the outcome of a repeated non-cooperative game played among sufficiently patient players may look as if it is the outcome of some cooperative process or some legally binding agreement to play cooperatively. Or, it may not. It all depends upon an intangible expectational factor that might legitimately be identified with the history or culture of the group of players.[38]

If each member of the group expects that every other member of the group will play cooperatively and that there will be a relatively severe penalty for not playing cooperatively, then the cooperative solution may become a self-reinforcing equilibrium. On the other hand, if members of the group expect that other members will not play cooperatively and the penalties for such behavior are relatively light, then a non-cooperative solution will emerge as a self-sustaining equilibrium. In general, there will be a continuum of infinitely many such solutions, ranging from more 'as if' cooperative to less 'as if' cooperative. It seems fair to identify a cooperative spirit or cooperative culture with a set of self-reinforcing expectations that result in a more 'as if' cooperative solution.

Let the outcome to a repeated non-cooperative prisoner's dilemma game be quantified by the parameter λ, which is valued between zero and one. A high value of λ near one means a non-cooperative solution that comes close to looking as if it were the outcome of cooperative collusion. A low value of λ near zero means a non-cooperative solution that is far from the cooperative solution, thus yielding low individual payoffs.

The parameter λ stands for the ability of a group of people to resolve prisoner's dilemma type free-riding problems internally, without the imposition of explicit rules of behavior, other things, including the size of the group, being equal.[39] With a value one of λ, people in a group would be able to resolve completely free riding problems internally, regardless of the size of the group. With a value zero of λ, even two people, the smallest group of people, cannot at all resolve free riding problems. With a value between zero and one of λ, people would be able to cooperate relatively effectively when their group is sufficiently small, but they may not be able to cooperate so effectively when their group is sufficiently large.

The relevant theory appears to allow taking λ as a more or less given function of culture. As we have readily admitted, it could be argued that our approach essentially shifts the paradox back one stage to explaining the determinants of λ. On balance, however, we think there is a useful net gain in understanding. A more serious inquiry would want to probe further, but suppose for the sake of argument we may temporarily treat λ as a quasi-fixed reduced form parameter. Of course it does not constitute proof, but a lot of anecdotal evidence could be cited to justify the general proposition that East Asia is a high-λ society relative to Europe, which by comparison is more of a low-λ society.[40] The entire topic of defining operationally a λ-value is worthy of further study. For the purposes of this paper, we merely wish to examine the likely relationship of various values of λ, taken as given, with property rights theory.

Ownership

It seems fair to say that the property rights literature is often presented as if it were culture-free, of universal applicability. Ownership gives a residual right to control an asset in the case of a missing contractual provision, thereby resolving potential conflicts and preventing shirking.[41] More generally, it is important to have well-defined property rights and clear reward systems of the right sort because otherwise there is an incentive for opportunistic and shirking behavior that can seriously undermine economic performance.

But if the way of looking at things presented in this paper has any validity, the significance of ownership interacts in a critical way with the ability to solve efficiently internal organizational problems without formal rules, which may perhaps be treated as more or less culturally given in many relevant cases. The orthodox version of property rights theory is not universal; it is really applicable only to a low-λ culture. With low values of λ, it becomes critically important to specify in detail the rules of ownership, rewards, and so forth, because without legally binding rules the low-λ organization will not achieve efficient results. On the other hand, formal property rights and binding legal rules become less important for a high-λ society relative to other issues like competition among organizations.

To give a specific example, let us look at so-called lock-in relationships or lock-in effects between parties, which are common in business practice. The lock-in effect refers to situations where a small number of parties make investments that are relationship-specific, i.e. once made, they have a much higher value inside the relationship than outside. For example, there is a lock-in effect between the firm and its workers when some of the workers' human capital invested today is firm-specific in the sense that their human capital payoff in the future depends on some particular features of their firm.

When there are lock-in effects, with a low value of λ, meaning people cannot trust each other, a long-term contract may be necessary to reduce opportunistic behavior or to induce people to formally cooperate by establishing legally the efficient lock-in relationship. However, if it is difficult or impossible to have a complete long-term contract between the parties, say because certain outcomes are unobservable or because the contract would be prohibitively costly to enforce, then overall ownership may be the necessary condition to maintain efficiency, since the owner of the physical assets, with the residual right or power of employing workers, can direct employees to utilize these assets in accordance with his directions.[42]

Making a group of people follow the instructions of other people is critical to the success of any large scale economic organization. In this sense, according to the property rights school, a well-defined ownership structure can be regarded as the necessary and unique instrument to make some people, the employees, follow the instructions of some other people, the owners, thereby avoiding potential conflicts in their joint pursuit of economic activities. In conventional property rights theory a low value of λ, or non-trusting behavior, is a fundamental assumption about the players of the game. It is so fundamental that economists simply do not mention it as an assumption.

Personally, we think it is plausible that in a society with a low value of λ the conventional property rights theory is essentially correct. However, if a society can be described by a high λ-value, or people trust each other, then without formal ownership parties may still be able to invest in the relationship or to lock together. In this case, it may not be necessary to have a well defined owner with a clear-cut right to exclude some people from accessing the asset. With a high λ, or a stronger capability for, or desirability of, cooperating, the threat of firing may not be necessary or may not be the best incentive for inducing good behavior. Put another way, well defined property rights may not be so crucial in a high-λ society. In any event, the existence of varying degrees of cooperating capabilities among people in disparate societies makes the importance of well-defined property rights itself vary across societies.

It seems to us that in a high λ-society, an implicit contract may be more efficient than an explicit contract. There may be many reasons for high-λ people to prefer implicit to explicit contracts.[43] First of all, there may be some saving of time and energy in negotiating, formulating, and enforcing the contract. There may also be an incentive effect of the implicit contract. If people are cooperative or can trust each other, employees may behave responsibly, as if they are residual claimants or owners, in the sense that they are willing to deal effectively with contingencies that may not be written or may not be able to be written in a formal contract. By contrast, in the case of an explicit contract, employees may do only those things specified in their employment contract. Thus, an implicit contract here may generate better incentives than an explicit contract.

In general, the costs of a contract, which include the costs of negotiation, observing or verifying outcomes, and enforcing the contract, are continuous rather than discrete. The value of λ across different societies is in principle also continuous, that is, people from different societies differ in their capability or desire to be cooperative. Thus, the costs and benefits of forming explicit contracts and implicit contracts will be different in different societies. There will be trade-offs between explicit contracts and implicit contracts. There may exist a range of situations where people who are more cooperative may prefer to have a gentleman's agreement, an implicit contract which is self-enforced by custom, good faith, and reputation, while low-λ people may need to have an explicit contract to prevent opportunistic behavior.

Concerning actual TVE contracts, law officials and policy makers report that such transactions are often based on oral agreements instead of written contracts. Even in the case of written contracts, it is often the case that the contracts are incomplete and unspecific in items, or there is no specific punishment for breaching the contract. It has been noted that part of the reason for the popularity of this kind of practice is the importance of long term relationships and connections for TVE transactions. (Liu (1989) "They regard friendship as the most secure way of doing business. They usually try to develop friendship first before doing business." (Cai (1990), p.201.) Given the importance of long term relationships and connections, when there are disputes many TVEs would rather settle privately instead of relying on the courts because they care more about keeping long-term connections, even though doing so may hurt their business in the short run.

6. SOME IMPLICATIONS OF A GENERALIZED PROPERTY RIGHTS THEORY

If the above story is believable, we have more or less answered the central paradox within the paradigm we have provided. Against the strong predictions of property rights theory, the Chinese model may succeed better in practice than the standard model because traditional property rights theory omits a critical variable and tends to treat only the low-λ case. In a high-λ society, the evolutionary Chinese model might be a better transition strategy because it may be less disruptive overall and it concentrates effort more directly on the main task of building market-oriented organizations. That these market-oriented organizations are ill-defined cooperatives may not be critically important. In a high-λ society the ownership structure can perhaps be sorted out later, if it even needs to be then. Perhaps China is headed more towards a high-λ Japanese-style capitalism than towards a low-λ European-style capitalism in any event.

As for the idea that a transforming country has the option of choosing between the Chinese and standard models, the framework of this paper seems to suggest that such choice may be largely illusory. If the ideas being put forth here are sound, the value of λ is essentially the product of a path-dependent historical heritage. The costs of changing culture are presumably very high, if culture is changeable at all. So it simply may not be a realistic option for Eastern Europe to be thinking in terms of the Chinese model. It may be that Eastern Europe really has no choice but to take the difficult route of developing and strengthening traditional private property rights appropriate to a low-λ society. By the same token, it is might not be fruitful for China or Vietnam or North Korea to be thinking in terms of the standard model. In a high-λ society, the time and effort needed to formalize property rights, contracts, and so forth is perhaps better spent on developing new products or on penetrating new markets or on increasing productivity or on other more directly productive activities.

The world is a complicated place and there may be many other contributing factors that explain the Chinese miracle. To the extent that these other factors are significant, the Chinese experience may have greater or lesser relevance to the Eastern European debates about the role of privatization and the speed of transformation. At the very minimum, the Chinese experience offers a strong counter-example to the sweeping claim, sometimes made in support of big bang approaches, that gradual reforms must fail.

The main purpose of this paper is to draw attention to the seemingly contradictory nature of the Chinese and standard approaches to transition. We have tried to argue strongly that TVEs are best viewed as vaguely defined cooperatives. The basic question of the paper then is: Why, given the usual emphasis by economists on the prime importance of well defined private property rights for incentives and for a successful transition from socialism to capitalism, should the Chinese township-village enterprises, which seem to operate under poorly defined property rights, have been so successful?

The second task of the paper tries to focus on a readily apparent explanation in terms of the ability to cooperate, or λ-value, of a society. This part is bound to be more controversial. Even if our explanation is largely true, there is still some question over how it might be applied. And there is no reason why all the countries of Eastern Europe should have the same λ-value. For example, it might be argued that Russia is more of an intermediate-λ society than most of the others. If so, there might be somewhat different policy implications for privatization for Russia than for the rest.

If the approach of this paper rings true, there is a lot of research remaining to be done. As it has been practiced thus far, the standard property rights theory seems to be covering only the low-λ case. How property rights theory interacts with the λ-value of an organization in the ore general case may prove to be an insightful way of viewing a number of issues.[44]

ENDNOTES

1. This chapter is co-authored with Martin L. Weitzman. It is reprinted with permission from *Journal of Comparative Economics*, **18**(2), 1994, published by the Academic Press. Copyright 1994 by the Academic Press. All rights reserved.

2. Some people may argue that, without a political revolution, China has only reforms and is not really making a true transition. But what we care about here is the essence of the change process, not its label.

3. The fundamental role of the TVE in Chinese reform has been recognized by many economists and policy makers. Deng Xiaoping admitted in 1987 that the amazing growth of the township and village enterprises was the greatest achievement of the reform and was completely unexpected (Chen, 1989).

4.See Lin (1987), Byrd and Lin (1990), Oi (1992), Nee (1992).

5. For example, Alchian and Demsetz (1972), Demsetz (1967), Furubotn and Pejovich (1974), Williamson (1985).

6. See,e.g., Grossman and Hart (1986), Hart and Moore (1990).

7. Alchian (1974), the founding father of the new property rights approach, admitted that the argument that private property rights are the precondition of a well-functioning market economy is a belief or a proposition which is "not yet

derivable from economic theory nor fully validated by sufficient evidence." In this section, we are summarizing property rights theory as a broad generalization or abstraction rather than an ironclad rule about how capitalist economies actually operate. In reality, there are some examples of public enterprises that outperform stagnant or failed private enterprises in the same industry. Also, there are some examples of regulation and even coercive government policies in capitalist economies that seem very successful.

8. Demsetz (1967), and Furubotn and Pejovich (1974).

9. Alchian and Demsetz (1972).

10. Kornai (1992).

11. By this time there is a sizable literature on transition economics. See, for example, the Fall 1991 symposium in *Journal of Economic Perspectives*.

12. Some of these are described in Stark (1992).

13. Many TVEs are located in urban areas. They are called TVEs simply because they are supervised by rural township or village governments and the majority of their employees are registered as rural laborers.

14. There are other forms of contracts in practice: the partnership contract, manager contract, and individual contract. In the partnership contract case, the executive owner, the community government, invites bids for the TVE. Individuals form partnership bidders. The winning partner signs a contract based on its bid with the community government. Then the manager is determined by the winning partner. In the manager contract or individual case, the manager or an individual signs a contract with the community government.

15. According to a sample survey conducted in 1986, 83.3 percent of township enterprise directors thought that they were appointed by the township government (Song (1990)).

16. The 75 percent% figure is from *China Statistical Yearbook, 1992*. Available data show that industrial TVEs are more efficient statically than the whole TVE sector in terms of labor profitability, while they are about equally efficient in terms of capital profitability. In 1989, an average employee in industrial TVEs earned 3,200 yuan of net after-tax profit, while an average employee in the whole TVE sector earned 2,500 yuan of net after-tax profit. Concerning capital profitability, the profit to capital ratio in industrial TVEs was 1.5, while it was 1.6 in the whole TVE sector. Calculations are based on data from *Chinese TVE Yearbook, 1990*, pp.128-136 and pp.187-191.

17. For studies bearing on TVE and SOE performance, see Chen *et al* (1988a, 1988b), Lau and Brada (1990), Svejnar (1990), Xu (1991), Jefferson *et al* (1992), Naughton (1993), Woo *et al* (1993). Some of the seemingly different results of these studies are due to a different underlying assumption about the relevant factor weights. For example, Jefferson *et al* use a labor share of 0.12, which significantly lowers their calculated TFP; if their data were reworked with a labor share of 0.7, results would be reasonably close to ours even though their capital series is differently derived.

18. The non-state sector's share of industrial output increased from 22 percent in 1978 to 47 percent in 1991, while the share of the state sector declined from 78 percent to 53 percent in the same period. In the non-state sector, about 4/5 of the output was produced by TVE and similar cooperatives. This pattern of change can alternatively be presented in specific real outputs. For example, in 1990, about 1/3 of coal, more than 1/4 of cement, about a half of electric fans, about 2/5 of canned food and paper, and about 4/5 of completed

construction projects in China were produced by the TVE sector. Exports by TVEs increased at an average annual rate of 66 percent from 1986 to 1990. All the numbers in this subsection are taken from *Statistical Yearbook of China, 1986 - 1992*.

19. Most managers of state enterprises interviewed by one of the authors in 1992 and 1993 in Beijing, Hebei, Guangdong, and Shanghai admitted that the most serious competition faced by the SOEs, which causes losses in many SOEs, comes from the TVEs, because of their competitive prices and quick adoption of innovations.

20. In a property rights experiment designed and implemented by the Regional Experiment Office of the State Council, TVEs in suburban Wenzhou were given the opportunity to clarify their ownership status. Somewhat surprisingly, it turned out that most TVEs did not wish to register as formal private firms under the legal protection of private property provided by the State Council. Instead, most TVEs insisted on registering as cooperatives or as township village enterprises (personal communication with Mai Lu, the former director of the Regional Experiment Office).

21. In their comparative studies of TVEs and other institutions throughout the world, Gelb and Svejnar (1990)also conclude that the institutions most similar to the Chinese TVE are producer cooperatives, including cooperatives in Eastern Europe, Mondragon enterprises in Spain, and labor managed firms in the former Yugoslavia.

22. In our interviews with managers of TVEs, they often acted surprised and even laughed when they were asked about the legal ownership status of the *cun-min*.

23. But even in this case, very often there is no share specified for the workers' investments in the TVE.

24. "National Academic Conference on TVE, 1984" in *China Agriculture Yearbook, 1984.*

25. Rural Policy Research Division of the Central Committee Secretariat,"A Summary of Nationwide Rural Socio-economic Sampling Survey," in *China Agricultural Yearbook, 1986.*

26. Article 4, Chapter 1, "The Stipulation of Contract Management Responsibility System in the TVE (*xiangzhen qiye chengbao jingying zeren zhi guiding*)."

27. According to the law, "more than or equal to 60 percent of the after-tax profit of an enterprise should be reserved for the enterprises' autonomous distribution. The reserved after-tax profit for the enterprise should be mainly used as investment funds for technological transformation and extending reproduction, and also as welfare funds and bonus funds in a proper way." (Article 32, Chapter 5, in *The PRC (People's Republic of China) Regulations of Rural Collectively-Owned Enterprises (RRCOE) (zhonghua renmin gonghehuo xiangcun jiti suoyou zhi qiye tiaoli)*, Beijing: People's Press. 1990.)).

28. "The share of the after-tax profit which is distributed to the owner should be used mainly for the construction of agricultural infrastructures, providing agriculture technology services, rural public welfare, and the renewal of enterprises or setting up of new enterprises." (Article 32, Chapter 5, in *The PRC (People's Republic of China) Regulations of Rural Collectively-Owned Enterprises (RRCOE) (zhonghua renmin gonghehuo xiangcun jiti suoyou zhi qiye tiaoli)*, Beijing: People's Press. 1990.)).

29. There are TVEs which are initiated and managed by individual entrepreneurs, and thus are not typical collectively-owned enterprises. But still the right of these TVEs to appropriate assets is very vague. The entrepreneurs borrow the land or other input factors from the community government.

As a condition of borrowing the land from the government, the enterprises have to be classified as collectively-owned enterprises even though the value of the TVE assets far exceeds the value the entrepreneurs borrowed from the government. Many do not know who is the real owner of the assets. Neither the community government nor the entrepreneur is the residual claimant of such firms.

30. By contrast, the separation of ownership and management in the typical capitalist firm at least allows equity owners the right to withdraw their shares from the firm in which they have invested if they are unhappy about the firm's performance. That is, genuine capitalist owners have the right to control their own investment.

31. For example, the law requires that "the owner should provide services for the production, supply and marketing of the enterprise, and *should respect the autonomy of the enterprise*"(emphases added). (Article 19, Chapter 3).

32. Personal interviews with officials of Guangdong provincial government and Shunde county government.

33. Personal interviews with managers of Beijao Township Corp., Rongqi Township Corp., Cuokou Village Corp. and officials of Shunde county in Guangdong province and Xianghe county in Hebei province.

34. *Zhongguo qiye guanli nianjian (China Enterprise Management Yearbook), 1990*, Beijing: Enterprise Management Press, 1990. p.342.

35. According to Mr. Gao Shangquan, Deputy Director of the State System Reform Committee of the State Council of China, in the early 1990's, there had been only 1/3 of state enterprises making profits, 1/3 making losses, and another 1/3 making *de facto* losses (The Keynote Speech at the Chinese Economic

Association (UK) 1992 Annual Conference, London).

36.David Kreps has formally developed a notion of corporate culture, some elements of which are similar to the ideas being exposited here. See Kreps (1990).

37. We assume basic familiarity with the prisoners' dilemma game. See, e.g., Fudenberg and Tirole (1992) and the references cited there.

38. The Folk theorem for infinitely repeated games can be summarized in the following terms (Fudenberg and Tirole (1991), pp.150-160): If the players discount the future at a sufficiently low rate, then individually rational payoffs can be supported by an equilibrium. Thus, in the limit of extreme patience, repeated play allows virtually any payoff to be an equilibrium outcome. Because multiple equilibria are generic in the repeated game, economists typically focus on cooperative results or efficient outcomes. But there is no generally accepted theoretical justification for assuming efficiency in this setting.

39. In TVEs, there is a popular spirit called "*gemen*" (buddy-ship commitment and loyalty), which plays an important role in substituting for formal rules, contracts or ownership. Some Chinese economists or businessman have noted that the *gemen* mechanism replaces contracts or ownership. A series of case studies in Anhui Province find that many TVEs consciously do not use formal contracts to maintain or to strengthen the *gemen* relationship, both in internal management and in outside transactions. People there "regard defining personal interests by written agreement or contracts as damaging "*gemen*" spirits." "In order to strengthen the atmosphere of stressing "*gemen*" spirit and downplaying personal interests inside the firm, ... managers earn not much more than workers" (Cai (1990), p.201).

40. It is possible to cite here some loose evidence to show that there are differences in cooperative behavior under different cultures, but such evidence would probably not convince anyone who did not want to be convinced, and the general subject seems well beyond the scope of this paper.

41. It has been argued that the residual right to control a property is the most important element of ownership. In addition to the right to decide the usage of the property except to the extent specified in a contract, ownership grants the right to exclude some people from accessing the property (Coase (1937), Grossman and Hart (1986), Hart and Moore (1990)).

42. General references are Coase, (1937), Williamson (1985), Grossman and Hart (1986), Hart and Moore (1990).

43. In the literature of contract theory, if a contract is not enforceable or prohibitively costly to enforce, the explicit contract will be given up or be replaced by an self-enforced implicit contract (Bull (1987), Hart and Holmstrom (1987)).

44. It was already mentioned that perhaps some aspects of Japanese-style capitalism might be illuminated by this approach.

Chapter 4

Risk Aversion, Rural-Urban Wage Differentiation, and Migration

1. INTRODUCTION

Two important related classical phenomena in most developing economies are the following: the coexistence of a high urban wage (in terms of the inability to clear the labor market) and a low rural wage in rural areas; and the coexistence of urban unemployment and the continuation of rural-urban migration.

In contrast, during the period of reform to transform the economy from a bureaucratically controlled to a market economy in China, the following interesting phenomena are observed: (i) compared with poor rural areas, more people in rich rural areas migrate to urban-suburban areas where wages are higher; (ii) people in poor rural areas migrate more to rich rural areas, where wages are higher than in poor rural areas but lower than in urban areas, than migrate to urban areas; while many rich rural area people migrate to urban areas; (iii) in many urban-suburban areas[1] with higher incomes than rural areas, insufficient migration phenomenon is observed. These phenomena cannot be explained by the existing theories.

To explain the classical paradoxical phenomena, many theories have been developed. The Leibenstein-Mirrlees-Stiglitz nutrition-based efficiency wage theory explains the rural-urban wage differential by linking food consumption and productivity. According to this theory, labor productivity is determined by the level of food consumption, which depends on the income of laborers. Thus, low incomes in poor rural areas result in low productivity and thus low income *per se*. And high income in urban areas is necessary for maintaining high productivity in themanufacturing industries (Leibenstein, 1957; Mirrlees, 1975; and Stiglitz, 1976). However, no strong evidence for the effect of food consumption on productivity exists to support this theory (Bliss and Stern, 1978; Strauss, 1986). Moreover, it was found in poor rural areas of India that real wages vary considerably across regions (Bliss and Stern, 1978; Rowsenzweig, 1984). Evidence also shows wage variations across Chinese rural areas (Xu, 1994). This wage variation contradicts the nutrition-wage theory which bases rural wages on stable biological needs.

The celebrated Harris-Todaro model and its variations (Corden and Findlay 1975; Cole and Sanders 1985; Harris and Todaro 1970; Stiglitz 1974; Todaro 1969) explain wage differentiations and rural-urban migration based on the hypothesis that rural people migrate to cities until expected urban incomes equal those of rural incomes. With the existence of unemployment in urban areas, in equilibrium expected wages should be the same in both rural and in urban areas.[2] According to the logic of this model, the poorer a rural area, the more rural-urban migration will occur. However, in China the number of rural-urban migrants from poor rural areas is less than those from rich rural areas (Geng, 1989). Moreover, there is a general trend, observed in most LDCs, that rural-urban migrants tend not to be from the poorest families in the original rural areas (Rowsenzweig, 1988, p.745).

Stark and Katz analyze the roles of risk aversion and imperfect capital markets in rural-urban migration (Katz and Stark, 1986; Stark, 1991). They argue that with fragmented capital markets, the rate of return on assets may be an increasing function of investment, which may result in a nonconvex acceptable gamble set even when an individual's utility function is strictly concave. Regarding migration as an investment, with a nonconvex acceptable gamble set, a risk-averse individual may take the risk of migration. This theory predicts that "the rural rich will not migrate." It contradicts the observation that rural-urban migrants tend not to be from poorer rural areas.

According to Lewis (1954) and Ranis and Fei (1961), the immobility of agricultural labor, which is responsible for the low income in rural areas, results from the discrepancy between theprivate and social costs of rural-urban migration. In rural areas, individuals get average agricultural products in the sense that they share agricultural products with their family members. However, with a labor surplus, each rural laborer's marginal labor productivity is much lower than the average labor productivity (they assume it to be zero or negative). Therefore, private cost of moving out of agriculture for an agricultural laborer, i.e. his/her average productivity in agriculture, is significantly higher than the social costs, which is his/her marginal product of labor in agriculture. The problems with these theories are the following: if household members are cooperative in the sense that they share the total income of the household such that the marginal utility of every member in the household is the same, a rational household should send laborers to urban areas to the point that the marginal products of labor in the city and in agriculture are the same. By so doing, the phenomenon of dual economies should disappear. If household members are not cooperative, the discrepancy between private and social costs of rural-urban migration should disapperar.

Like other developing countries, in Chinese rural areas, labor is the most abundant resource: both the marginal product of labor and labor income in agriculture are much lower than those of manufacturing and other industries in the cities. However, during the period ofthe economic reforms, many interesting but not well understood features of China's rural-urban migration are observed: migration from poorer rural areas (e.g. West China) is lower than migration from richer rural areas (e.g. East China)

(Geng, 1989). Related to this, the insufficient migration phenomenon is observed in many urban-suburban areas where "rural industrial enterprises" are heavily concentrated: (i) in many suburban areas industrial enterprises have exhausted the local labor force and there are insufficient immigrants to meet labor demands, even though wages in these enterprises are higher than agricultural incomes in most areas (Byrd and Lin, 1990; Chen, 1987); (ii) in many sample surveys, managers of enterprises complained about labor shortage problems (Lin, 1987); (iii) an econometric study finds that the marginal product of labor of the enterprises in many urban-suburban areas is significantly higher than their wages (Xu, 1994). This suggests that an insufficient labor supply may result in the inefficient operation of these enterprises.

The puzzling questions are: why do people in poor rural areas, where surplus laborers result in serious low marginal labor productivities, migrate less than people in rich rural areas to urban areas? Why do many people in poor rural areas migrate to rich rural areas where wages are lower than urban wages, while many rich rural area people migrate to urban areas?

This paper provides a theory to explain these phenomena. The theory is based on the feature of the risks faced by out-migrants and their families -- regarding rural households as geographically extended cooperative families.

Facing high risks of price fluctuations for basic needs, such as housing and food (in the rest part of the paper we use food prices as an example), a geographically extended cooperative household which has land and has out-migrants regards city jobs as high-risk high-income opportunities, and regards agricultural production on its own land as low-risk low-income opportunities. Because agricultural outputs from their land are not affected by price fluctuations, agricultural production serves as an insurance for rural households: in a bad year, the household will be able to survive by relying on their agricultural output. In order to insure themselves, risk-averse rural households would keep more labor input in agriculture (i.e. they reduce the number of rural-urban migrants) compared with risk-neutral households. Therefore, the "excess" labor input in agriculture and the resulting lower marginal labor productivity in agricultural production is virtually the payment for the insurance of rural households.

Regarding migration as an instrument of the income portfolio of a household, in an economy where most rural households have land, if poorer households are more risk-averse than rich households, then with respect to their insurance, a poor rural household will have fewer rural-urban migrants than a rich rural household. With safer real incomes in agricultural jobs, many members of households in poor rural areas migrate to rich rural areas, up to the point that the marginal labor productivities in the poor areas equal those in the rich areas. An important implication of this result is that the gap between the poor and the rich is widened when there are opportunities for rural laborers to migrate to cities, and migration provides more chances to earn higher incomes.

With respect to the influence of taxation on urban-rural migration, I show that a real land tax virtually reduces the insurance of rural households, and thus reduces rural-urban migration; the higher the tax, the fewer the migrants. With high real land taxes in China, rural-urban migration is further restricted.

For the migration problem of landless rural households, I show that under some conditions all members of landless households migrate to cities. This result may provide some clues for the differences between a reformed Chinese economy and some other developing economies: in China, almost all rural households have land, rural-urban migrants face big uncertainties in the free markets, and insufficient rural-urban migration is observed; in other developing countries, a notable number of rural households are landless, rural-urban migrants are not as clearly differentiated from other urban residents in the markets as they are in China, and migration-related unemployment is a distinguishing feature. When there are many landless rural households and the marginal labor productivity in agriculture is very low, the Harris-Todaro model is a good approximation of the rural-urban migration phenomenon. However, it is not a proper model for the case where most rural households have cropland regardless of the marginal labor productivity level in agriculture.

The rest of the paper is organized as follows: Section 2 provides the evidence for the analysis. Section 3 discusses the basic model and Section 4 extends the model to the economy where there are poor rural areas and rich rural areas.

2. INSUFFICIENT RURAL-URBAN MIGRATION: EVIDENCE

(A) In Poor Rural Areas There Are More Rural-Rural Migrants but Less Rural-Urban Migrants than in Rich Rural Areas

A sample survey conducted in seven counties in Henan province shows that the number of rural-urban migrants is positively correlated to per-capita grain production (Hou et al., 1988); that is, the more grain production, the more rural-urban migration.

The Figure 1 is based on data from a sample survey of more than two hundred villages in forty-nine counties of ten provinces.[3] The figure shows that rural-urban labor migration is positively correlated with per-capita agricultural income, and that net rural-rural labor migration is negatively correlated with per-capita agricultural income. (It is interesting to note from the figure that in regions with a per-capita agricultural income higher than 600 yuan there is a net immigration from other rural areas.

But in regions with a per-capita agricultural income lower than 500 yuan, there is a net rural-rural out-migration.)

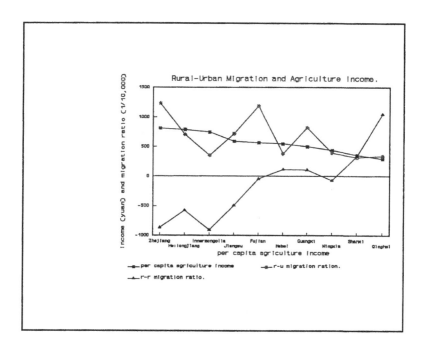

Figure 1. Rural Migration and Agricultural Income.

Chen (1987) estimates that by the mid-1980s some six million laborers each year were leaving poor rural areas for rich rural areas, and that up to 1987 close to 20 percent of the laborers in some poor villages had departed. One example is the rural-rural migration from poor rural areas to Baoan county of Guangdong province which is a rich rural area. Close to Shenzhen Special Economic Zone, most rural laborers in Baoan have taken nonagricultural work in the city. They rent out their land to immigrant laborers. According to official reports, by April

1986 the number of temporary immigrant laborers accounted for 60 percent of the resident population in that area (Wu and Xu, 1990).

(B) Crop Land as an Insurance Instrument for Rural Households

In China, the government differentiates immigrants with rural origins from city residents through the so-called household registration system: only city residents are eligible for access to almost-free state-owned residential housing and to buy grain products in state-owned food stores.[4] Immigrants with rural origins have to rely on free markets for their housing and grain consumption, although they can earn a higher nominal income compared to rural laborers and even compared to some urban laborers.

Table 1. Land in the Households of TVE Employees
(in percentages)

0 mu	1-5 mu	6-10 mu	11 mu and more
3.8	27.8	31.6	36.8

Source: Lin (1987).

In order to reduce the dependency on the unstable free market for food consumption, rural households with TVE employees may want to keep their cropland as insurance. However, the land may become a burden for out-migration.

Sample surveys show that 96.2 percent of TVE employees keep cropland at home.

An opinion survey shows that rural households explicity regard cropland as an insurance instrument. In the survey, 86 percent of the TVE employees said that they would like to keep the land in their household for safety reasons; all of them said that with cropland in their households, losing their current nonagricultural jobs would not affect the basic life of their families. Among the sample of rural laborers who were doing agricultural work, 45 percent of them did not want to migrate to cities, since they did not feel safe to leave their land; 80 percent of wanted to find a non-agricultural job in the local area without leaving their land; and among the people who wanted to find nonagricultural jobs in the local area, 91 percent wanted to keep their land even after they got a nonagricultural job (Hou et al., 1988).

(C) Insufficient Immigrants in China's Urban-Suburban Areas

Several case studies and sample surveys from more than one dozen counties (e.g., Jiangyin County in Jiangsu and Zhongshan county in Guangdong, etc.) find that in many newly industrialized areas the local labor force is exhausted, and insufficient migration has been a problem for further development. Under this situation, many firms have begun to adopt capital intensive technologies (He, 1990).

In an opinion survey conducted in Shanxi province, 47.4 percent of the TVE managers complained about the labor shortage problem. According to their responses, the local labor force was exhausted with the development of the local TVEs and this has caused labor shortages (Lin, 1987).

In the suburbs of Suzhou, Wuxi and Changshu, 59.27 percent of the rural labor force was working in nonagricultural sectors. In these areas, almost all of the younger labor force was already working in nonagricultural sectors. "The labor shortage is a prevailing phenomenon in these areas." Most employees of the TVEs lived less than twenty km away, because they wanted to go home regularly to take care of their land (Chen, 1987).

An econometric study finds that the marginal product of labor in the TVEs (township village enterprises)[5] is significantly higher than their wages (Xu, 1994). This suggests that TVEs do not earn as high profits as they could earn if they hired more laborers.

3. RURAL-URBAN MIGRATION: THE BASIC MODEL

The basic features of the model are the following: (i) the decision-making unit is the household. A household in this paper is regarded as a geographically extended family which can be quite large. Members in a household are perfectly cooperative in the sense that they share the total real income and risks in a egalitarian way such that everybody's marginal utility is the same; (ii) households are risk-averse; (iii) there are random shocks to the prices of basic needs, such as housing and food. In the rest of the paper, we mention only food prices. This is only for the sake of presentation.   Suppose that there are two states of nature in food price σ: good states and bad states.[6] Prices in the economy are expressed as $\mathbf{P}=\{P_a, P_m\}$. Here, P_a is the price of the agricultural good and P_m is the price of the manufactured good. The prices in different states are expressed as follows:

(1)   prices in a good state $\mathbf{P}(\sigma=g) = \mathbf{P}^* = \{p^*, p_m^*\}$,

with $\Pr.(\sigma=g) = q$;

prices in a bad state $\mathbf{P}(\sigma=b) = \underline{\mathbf{P}} = \{\underline{p}, \underline{p}_m\}$, with $\Pr.(\sigma=b) = 1-q$.

In this paper, I assume that there is an exogenously given urban wage ceiling and it is binding.[7]

To simplify the analysis, assume urban wage w remains constant in both states,[8] and two par cases in a bad state are analyzed: (i) both prices increase by the same factor $\beta > 1$; and (ii) the manufactured good price does not change, i.e. $p_m^* = \underline{p}_m = 1$.

The economy consists of a large number of identical households each with a population M. In this economy, all of the population are laborers. Here, M is quite large since a household is regarded as an extended family. Each household is endowed with the same amount of land and capital. The only choice variable of a household is labor: the allocation of labor endowment in agriculture and in the cities. The agricultural production function of every household is the same and is expressed as $f(N)$. Here, N is the labor input of agricultural production. Assume that land is limited such that changing the labor input will not change the area of land cultivated, i.e. there is a labor surplus in agricultural production, therefore $L = \underline{L} = $ constant. Agricultural production technology $f()$ satisfies the following properties: $f' > 0$ and $f'' < 0$ (decreasing return to scale).

In general, there are μ members of a household who migrate to cities. Members of a household are perfectly cooperative, that is they share the total income and they share the risks. The incomes of a household with μ members migrating to cities in different states are the following:

(2)   in a good state: $I(\mu, \mathbf{P}^*) = p^* f(M-\mu) + \mu w$;

in a bad state: $I(\mu, \underline{\mathbf{P}}) = \underline{p} f(M-\mu) + \mu w$.

where w is the exogenously given nominal urban wage.

For one household, μ is an integer. However, when the total number of households in the model is very large, regarding μ as an average number of migrants for each household, then μ

is a real number.

The expected indirect utility of a household is the following:

$$U(\mu;\sigma) = qU(\mathbf{P}^*,I(\mu,\mathbf{P}^*)) + (1-q)U(\underline{\mathbf{P}},I(\mu,\underline{\mathbf{P}})). \qquad (3)$$

The indirect utility function is defined as follows:

$$U(\mathbf{P},I(\mu,\mathbf{P}))$$

$$= V(X(\mathbf{P},I(\mu,\mathbf{P}))$$

$$= \text{max. } V(X_a, X_m)$$

$$\text{s.t. } P_a(\sigma)X_a + P_m(\sigma)X_m = I. \qquad (4)$$

Here, X_m and X_a are the consumption of the manufactured good and the agricultural good respectively, $P_a(\sigma)$ is the price of the agricultural good in state σ, and $P_m(\sigma)$ is the price of the manufactured good in state σ. To facilitate the analysis, assume that the utility function is differentiable and strictly concave, and satisfies the following conditions: $\partial U/\partial p_a < 0$, $\partial^2 U/\partial p_a^2 \geq 0$, $\partial U/\partial I > 0$, $\partial^2 U/\partial I^2 \leq 0$, $\partial^2 U/\partial I \partial P_i(\sigma) \leq 0$.

Assumptions on parameters:

(a) $w/p^* > f'(0)$ (in a good state, the real city wage for rural immigrants is higher than the highest possible marginal agricultural income);[9]

(b) $w/\underline{p} < f'(M)$ (in a bad state, the real city wage for rural immigrants is lower than the lowest possible marginal agricultural income).[10]

The household migration problem can be expressed as follows:

(5) Max. $qU(\mathbf{P}^*,p^*f(M-\mu)+\mu w) + (1-q)U(\underline{\mathbf{P}},\underline{p}f(M-\mu)+\mu w)$.
   μ

The FOC of problem (5) is that

(6) $\Phi= qU_I(\mathbf{P}^*,I(\mu^*,\mathbf{P}^*))(w-p^*f'(M-\mu^*))$

         $+(1-q)U_I(\underline{\mathbf{P}},I(\mu^*,\underline{\mathbf{P}}))(w-\underline{p}f'(M-\mu^*))$

    $= 0.$

Here, $U_I(\mathbf{P},I(\mathbf{P}))=\partial U(\mathbf{P},I(\mathbf{P}))/\partial I(\mathbf{P})$.

It can be easily shown that the household problem (5) is concave. Thus, given the fact that the migration must be in the interval of 0 and m (the total number of family members), for a risk-averse household with decreasing returns agricultural technology, the household has a unique optimal migration solution μ^*.

Proposition 1: (i) In the $\underline{p}_m=\beta p_m$, $\underline{p}=\beta p$, and w=const case, a risk-neutral rural household will allocate its laborers in such a way that its expected marginal product of labor equals the expected urban wage;

(ii) in the $p_m=\underline{p}_m=1$ case, the migration from a risk-neutral rural household will be reduced (or its laborers kept in the rural area will be increased) such that its expected marginal product of labor is lower than the expected urban wage;

(iii) everything else being equal, a household with a higher degree of risk aversion will have fewer rural-urban migrants, i.e. $d\mu/dr<0$.

Proof: see Appendix.

Proposition 1 implies that the number of rural-urban migrants from risk-averse households will be less than the number from risk-neutral households. Moreover, the number of agricultural laborers in risk-averse households will be more than the number in risk-neutral households so that the expected marginal product of labor in agriculture will be lower than the expected city wage.

Proposition 1(i) shows that when households are risk-neutral and when there is no change in relative price, then the model degenerates into the Harris-Todaro model and has the same result: expected income in cities should be the same as in agriculture. Proposition 1(ii) shows that even for a risk-neutral case, if there is a relative price shock, then migration will be less than what the Harris-Todaro model predicts.

Proposition 1(iii) is the general case -- risk-averse households, i.e. $r > 0$. In this general case, rural-urban migration will be lower than that predicted by the Harris-Todaro model, and expected city income will be higher than the expected agricultural income. That is because risk-averse households care more about risks than risk-neutral households. Under this condition, in order to ease the negative effect of random shocks, risk-averse households will allocate more laborers to agriculture than will risk-neutral households. This result is consistent with the following observed important phenomenon: the expected city wage is higher than the expected agricultural income, i.e. rural-urban migration is not sufficient in the sense of the Harris-Todaro model and its variations:

Compared with the result from the Harris-Todaro model, this model predicts that there is a labor surplus in agriculture in the sense that the expected marginal product of labor is lower than that in the Harris-Todaro model. Here, the excess labor input in agriculture is an insurance arrangement for rural households. Even though there are city jobs with high wages, rural households rationally choose to limit their out-migrants. This limitation of rural-urban migration results in an expected-wage differentiation between rural areas and urban areas.

This explanation of rural-urban migration and of the rural-urban wage differentiation is based on the features of the risks faced by rural households and the risk-averse preferences of rural households. This theory is different from the popular explanations for rural-urban migration and wage differentiation in developing economies (for other popular explanations, see Harris and Todaro, 1970; Jorgenson, 1967; Lebenstein, 1957; Lewis,1954; Mirrlees, 1975; Ranis and Fei, 1961; Sen, 1966; and Stiglitz, 1976, etc.).

It is a common observation that the influence of a random shock may be larger on a poor household than on a rich household. This is because survival is more serious for a poor household when there is a random shock. For a rich household, surviving *per se* may not be a problem. As a result, a poor household may be more risk-averse than a rich household. Denoting poor and rich by subscript p and r respectively, this phenomenon can be described as $r_p(.) > r_r(.)$. Under this assumption, Proposition 2 predicts that, for whatever reasons, if a household is poorer than others, then the number of rural-urban migrants from this household will be fewer than from the number other households.

Corollary: If $r_p(.) > r_r(.)$, then a poorer household has fewer rural-urban migrants than a richer household.[11]

This corollary is consistent with the empirical evidence found in China, where there are fewer rural-urban migrants from poor provinces than there are from rich provinces (Geng, 1989). An important implication of this result is that the poor become poorer and the rich become richer when there are opportunities for rural laborers to migrate to cities, and migration provides better chances to earn higher incomes.

Proposition 3:   (i) When households are more optimistic about the state of nature, i.e. when q increases, rural-urban migration will increase, i.e. $d\mu/dq > 0$;

(ii) when the agricultural-product price in a good state p increases, rural-urban migration will decrease, i.e.

dµ/dp<0;

(iii) when the agricultural-product price in a bad state p increases, if rural households are risk-neutral or almost risk-neutral (the ARA is very small), rural-urban migration will decrease, i.e. dµ/dp<0; if rural households are risk-averse, when p increases, rural-urban migration may or may not decrease, i.e. dµ/dp is indeterminate.

Proof: see Appendix.

A policy implication of Propositions 2 and 3 is that stabilizing food prices in the free markets, or providing food insurance for rural-urban migrants, especially for those from poor rural households, is helpful to increase labor mobility between rural and urban areas, to reduce rural-urban wage differentiations, and to prevent a widening of the gap between rich and poor areas.

In explaining urbanization or rural-urban migration, there have been two principal competing theories advanced in the literature: the population-push theory and the urban-pull theory (Williamson, 1988). The population-push theory claims that population growth pressing on limited farm land pushes rural laborers into the cities (Ravenstein, 1889; Lewis, 1954). The urban-pull theory maintains that higher wages associated with the development of industries in urban areas pull migrants into cities (Engels, 1845, 1974). In the following, proposition 4 analyzes the urban-pull effect and proposition 5 examines the population-push effect on rural-urban migration.

Proposition 4: (i) If households are risk-neutral or almost risk-neutral (i.e. the ARA is very small), when the urban wage increases, rural-urban migration increases, i.e. dµ/dw>0;

(ii) if there are very few rural-urban migrants, when the urban wage increases, rural-urban migration increases regardless of the degree of risk aversion of the households, i.e. if µ is very small, dµ/dw>0;

(iii) if households are risk-averse and the number of rural-urban migrants is not too few, when the urban wage increases, the rural-urban migration may or may not increase, i.e. sign (dμ/dw) is ambiguous.

Proof: see Appendix.

If there are very few rural-urban migrants, or if rural households are risk neutral or slightly risk-averse, with other things being equal, the urban-pull effect will be significant: an increase of the urban wage pulls more migrants from the rural areas. However, when there are already quite a few rural-urban migrants, and when rural households are risk-averse, the urban-pull effect may or may not exist. More specifically, under the condition that the real urban wage is much higher than the agricultural marginal labor productivity in a good state and that the subjective probability of the state being good is high, i.e. if q, r, μ, and w-p*f' are large, then when the city wage increases, rural households increase the number of laborers in agriculture to strengthen their insurance by reducing the number of migrants. This is because a very risk-averse household may want to buy more insurance (increasing laborers in agricuture) when the household has a higher income (city wages increase and the household already has quite a few members in the cities).

In most developing economies, or at early stages of industrialization, the number of rural-urban migrants is few compared with that of the rural population. Thus, the urban-pull effect is significant. However, when there are many rural-urban migrants, the urban-pull effect may not be significant.

Proposition 5: (i) For risk-neutral or almost risk-neutral households (i.e. the ARA is very small), when the population of these households increase, rural-urban migration also increases, i.e. dμ/dm>0;

(ii) if agricultural technology exhibits strongly decreasing returns to scale and the marginal product of labor is very low, when the rural population increases, rural-urban migration also increases regardless of the degree of risk aversion of the rural households, i.e. if f" << 0, and f'→0, then dμ/dm>0;

(iii) if agricultural technology does not exhibit strongly decreasing returns to scale and the marginal product of labor is not low, when the population in risk-averse households increases, rural-urban migration may or may not increase, i.e. dμ/dm is indeterminate.

Proof: see Appendix.

When the marginal product of labor in agriculture is almost zero,[12] or rural households are risk neutral or slightly risk-averse, with other things being equal, the population-push effect will be significant: a population increase in rural households pushes more migrants to urban areas. However, when rural households are risk-averse and the marginal product of labor in agriculture is not too low, the population-pull effect may or may not exist. More specifically, with high risk aversion and pessimistic households, under the condition that the urban wage is already much higher than the marginal product of labor in agriculture and the degree of decreasing returns in agricultural production is not high, i.e. if q, r, and w-p*f' are sufficiently large, and the absolute value of f" is not large, then when the population m increases, these households increase the number of laborers in agriculture to strengthen their insurance by reducing migration. This is because with a low cost of insurance (a low degree of decreasing returns in agricultural production) and a reasonably high income, when the endowment of a household increases, the risk-averse and pessimistic household may want to buy more insurance.

4. RURAL-RURAL AND
RURAL-URBAN MIGRATION

In addition to migrating to urban areas, when there are rich and poor rural areas there may also be rural-rural migration: people from a poor rural area may migrate to a rich rural area. Thus, households in poor rural areas have three portfolio instruments: stay on their own land, migrate to rich rural areas, migrate to urban areas.

According to the Harris-Todaro model, if wages in a rich rural area are lower than in the urban areas, people in both rich and poor rural areas should migrate to urban areas. Moreover, people in poor rural areas should migrate more to urban areas than people in rich rural areas. However, casual evidence shows that in China many more people in poor rural areas migrate to rich rural areas than to urban areas, while people in rich rural areas migrate to urban areas. This phenomenon itself contributes to the insufficient rural-urban migration and needs to be explained. In this section, the basic model is extended to analyze this phenomenon.

To simplify the analysis, only one polar case is analyzed, i.e. the case where both prices π_a and π_m increase by the same factor $\beta > 1$ in a bad state. Moreover, I assume that rural households in all rural areas are the same except that the technology in a poor area is less productive than the technology in a rich area. That is, the prosperity of rural areas is determined by exogenous factors (e.g. land quality or other technical factors). Agricultural production technologies with a labor input of N in rich and poor rural areas are described by the production functions $f_r(N)$ and $f_p(N)$ respectively. f_r and f_p satisfy the following properties: $f_r(N) > f_p(N)$, $f_r'(N) > f_p'(N) > 0$, $f_r''(N) < 0$ and $f_p''(N) < 0$. Assumptions (a) and (b) on the parameters in Section 3 are the same.

The income of a rural-rural migrant is the marginal product of his/her labor on rented land.[13]   Moreover, this agricultural income is real, as opposed to the city wage which is nominal. The income of a rich rural household from its land is the total output of its land minus the payment to the hired migrants. Members of households both in rich rural areas and in poor areas may migrate to urban areas. Assume that the city wage level is exogenously given and is not indexed.[14] The income of a poor household I_p is the summation of the agricultural income from its own land (total output) and the income from rural-rural migrants (marginal products of labor), as well as the income from rural-urban migrants (wages). The income of a rich household I_r is the summation of the agricultural income from its own land (total output minus the salary to migrants), and the income from rural-urban migrants (wages). Formally, I_p and I_r in different states are the following:

$$I_p(n,\mu_p,\mathbf{P^*})=p[f_p(M-n-\mu_p)+nf_r'(n_r+M-\mu_r)]+\mu_p w;$$

$$I_p(n,\mu_p,\underline{\mathbf{P}})=\underline{p}[f_p(M-n-\mu_p)+nf_r'(n_r+M-\mu_r)]+\mu_p w;$$

$$I_r(\mu_r,\mathbf{P^*})=p[f_r(n_r+M-\mu_r)-n_r f_r'(n_r+M-\mu_r)]+\mu_r w;$$

$$I_r(\mu_r,\underline{\mathbf{P}})=\underline{p}[f_r(n_r+M-\mu_r)-n_r f_r'(n_r+M-\mu_r)]+\mu_r w.$$

Here, μ_p and μ_r are the numbers of rural-urban migrants originally from poor areas and from rich areas respectively, n is the number of rural-rural migrants from poor rural households, n_r is the number of migrant laborers hired by rich households. n_r is collectively determined by the labor market. For a single rich household, it is exogenously given.

The expected indirect utilities of a rich household and a poor household are the following respectively:

$$U^r(\mu_r) = qU(\mathbf{P^*},I_r(\mu_r,\mathbf{P^*})) + (1-q)U(\underline{\mathbf{P}},I_r(\mu_r,\underline{\mathbf{P}}));$$

$$U^P(n,\mu_p) = qU(\mathbf{P}^*,I_p(n,\mu_p,\mathbf{P}^*)) + (1-q)U(\underline{\mathbf{P}},I_p(n,\mu_p,\underline{\mathbf{P}})).$$

Here, the expected utility function is defined as follows:

$$U(p_a,I(\mu,p_a)) = V(X(p_a,I(\mu,p_a))).$$

Here, $U(.)$ satisfies the following properties: $\partial U/\partial p < 0$, $\partial^2 U/\partial p^2 \geq 0$, $\partial U/\partial I > 0$, $\partial^2 U/\partial I^2 \leq 0$, and $\partial^2 U/\partial I \partial \pi_i(\sigma) \leq 0$.

The rich rural household migration problem is basically the same as the basic model. In the following, I concentrate on the poor rural household migration problem.

A poor rural household chooses the number of rural-rural migrants and the number of rural-urban migrants to maximize its expected utility, given that a rich rural household chooses the number of rural-urban migrants to maximize its expected utility.

The migration problem for a household in a poor area is the following:

Max. $qU(\mathbf{P}^*,p[f_p(M-n-\mu_p)+nf_r{}'(n_r+M-\mu_r)]+\mu_p w)$
n,μ_p

$\qquad + (1-q)U(\underline{\mathbf{P}},\underline{p}[f_p(M-n-\mu_p)$

$\qquad +nf_r{}'(n_r+M-\mu_r)]+\mu_p w).$ $\qquad\qquad$ (7)

s.t. $\mu_r = $ argmax. U^r

$\qquad = qU(\mathbf{P}^*,p[f_r(n_r+M-\mu_r)-n_rf_r{}'(n_r+M-\mu_r)]+\mu_r w$

$\qquad + (1-q)U(\underline{\mathbf{P}},\underline{p}[f_r(n_r+M-\mu_r)$

$\qquad - n_rf_r{}'(n_r+M-\mu_r)]+\mu_r w).$ $\qquad\qquad$ (8)

(8) can be replaced by its FOC as follows:

$$qU_I(w-p^*f_r'(n_r+M-\mu_r)+n_rp^*f_r''(n_r+M-\mu_r))$$

$$+ (1-q)U_I(w-\underline{p}f_r'(n_r+M-\mu_r)+n_r\underline{p}f_r''(n_r+M-\mu_r))=0. \qquad (8a)$$

The FOCs of problem (7) are the following:

$$\partial U/\partial n = [qU_{I}p+(1-q)U_{I}\underline{p}][f_r'(n_r+M-\mu_r)-f_p'(M-n^*-\mu_p^*)]$$

$$= 0, \qquad (9)$$

or,

$$f_r'(n_r+M-\mu_r)=f_p'(M-n^*-\mu_p^*). \qquad (9')$$

And,

$$\partial U/\partial\mu_p = qu_I(w-p^*f_p'(M-n^*-\mu_p^*))$$

$$+ (1-q)U_I(w-\underline{p}f_p'(M-n^*-\mu_p^*))$$

$$= 0. \qquad (10)$$

Proposition 6: For risk-averse households with decreasing returns from agricultural technologies, the household migration problem (7) has a unique solution $\{\mu_p^*, n^*\}$.

Proof: see Appendix.

It is easy to see from the first order condition (9') that in equilibrium there is migration from poor rural areas to rich rural areas and urban areas such that the marginal product of labor in poor rural areas is equal to that in rich areas.

Proposition 7: For a rural household in a poor rural area where there are opportunities to migrate to rich rural areas and urban areas,

(i) when the rural household is risk-neutral, it will allocate its laborers, which include rural-rural migrants, rural-urban migrants, and laborers at home, in such a way that the expected marginal product of labor equals the expected urban wage;

(ii) as the household becomes more risk-averse, the number of rural-urban migrants in the household will decrease, i.e. $d\mu_p/dr<0$;

(iii) when the household becomes more risk-averse, the number of rural-rural migrants in the household will increase, i.e. $dn/dr>0$;

(iv) the number of rural-urban migrants from poor rural areas is less than the number from rich areas, i.e. $\mu_r>\mu_p$;

(v) compared with people from rich rural areas, people from poor rural areas are more likely to work in agriculture, i.e. $m-\mu_r < m-\mu_p$.

Proof: see Appendix.

Proposition 8: For a risk-averse rural household in a poor rural area where there are opportunities to migrate to rich rural areas and urban areas, we have the following results:

(i) when the agricultural-product price in a good state p increases, rural-rural migration increases and rural-urban migration decreases, i.e. $\partial n/\partial p > 0$ and $\partial\mu_p/\partial p < 0$;

(ii) when the agricultural-product price in a bad state p increases, rural-rural migration increases and rural-urban migration decreases, i.e. $\partial n/\partial\underline{p} > 0$ and $\partial\mu_p/\partial\underline{p} < 0$;

(iii) when the poor household is more optimistic about the state of nature, i.e. when the subjective probability q increases, rural-rural migration decreases and rural-urban migration increases, i.e. $\partial n/\partial q < 0$ and $\partial\mu_p/\partial q > 0$.

Proof: see Appendix.

Proposition 9: (i) For a risk-neutral or almost risk-neutral poor rural household (i.e. the ARA is almost 0), when the city wage increases, rural-rural migration decreases and rural-urban migration increases, i.e. $dn/dw<0$ and $d\mu_p/w > 0$;

(ii) if there are very few rural-urban migrants, when the urban wage increases, rural-urban migration increases and rural-rural migration decreases regardless of the degree of risk aversion of the households, i.e. if μ_p is very small, $dn/dw<0$ and $d\mu_p/w > 0$;

(iii) for a risk-averse poor rural household, when the city wage increases, rural-rural migration may or may not decrease, i.e. dn/dw is ambiguous. Moreover, the change of rural-urban migration is in the opposite direction of dn/dw, i.e. sign $d\mu_p/dw =$ sign $-dn/dw$ is also ambiguous.

Proof: see Appendix.

Proposition 10: (i) For a risk-neutral or almost risk-neutral poor rural household, if production in a rich area shows stronger decreasing returns to scale than in a poor area, i.e. $f_r''\leq f_p''$, then when the population of a household increases, rural-rural migration decreases and rural-urban migration increases, i.e. $\partial n/\partial m < 0$ and $\partial \mu_p/\partial m > 0$;

(ii) if the agricultural technology in a poor area exhibits strong decreasing returns to scale and the marginal product of labor is very low, and if production in a rich area shows a stronger decreasing return to scale than in a poor area, i.e. $f_r''\leq f_p''$, when the rural population increases, rural-rural migration decreases and rural-urban migration increases regardless of the degree of risk aversion of the rural households, i.e. if $f_p'' << 0$, and $f_p' \rightarrow 0$, then $\partial n/\partial m < 0$ and $\partial \mu_p/\partial m > 0$;

(iii) in general, when the population of a household increases, rural-rural migration may or may not increase, i.e $\partial n/\partial m$ is ambiguous. Moreover, sign $\partial \mu_p/\partial m$ is also ambiguous.

Proof: see Appendix.

5. APPLICATION OF THE MODEL:
LAND TAX AND LANDLESS HOUSEHOLDS

Land Tax

Some taxation under certain circumstances may affect rural-urban migration. In the following, the model is employed to analyze the effect of land taxes on rural-urban migration. Land taxes in this model are taxes imposed on a rural household solely based on the area cultivated in agricultural production. Two kinds of land taxes are analyzed: a monetary land tax and a real land tax.[15]

With a monetary or a nominal land tax, the incomes of households in different states are the following:

$I(\mathbf{P^*})=p^*f(M-\mu)+\mu w-t;$

$I(\underline{\mathbf{P}})=\underline{p}f(M-\mu)+\mu w-t.$

Proposition 11: With a nominal land tax t,

(i) if rural households are risk-neutral, or have a constant ARA, then the nominal tax has no effect on rural-urban migration, i.e. $d\mu/dt=0$;

(ii) if households are less risk-averse in a good state than in a bad state, i.e. if $r(\mathbf{P^*},I(\mathbf{P^*}))<r(\underline{\mathbf{P}},I(\underline{\mathbf{P}}))$, then when the nominal tax increases, rural-urban migration will decrease, i.e. $d\mu/dt<0$.

Proof: see Appendix.

A fixed nominal tax is lighter in a bad year (when the

nominal agricultural income is higher) than in a good year (when the nominal agricultural income is lower). The effect of a nominal land tax on rural-urban migration does not depend on the level of risk aversion of the rural households, but depends on the risk-aversion gap between a bad state and a good state. The higher the degree of risk aversion in a bad state over that in a good state, the larger the effect of the tax on migration. If risk aversion is independent of the stats, a nominal land tax has no effect on rural-urban migriation.

However, with a real land tax or a land tax in kind, the effect of the tax on migration will be different. In this case, the incomes of households in different states are the following:

$$I(\mathbf{P}^*)=p[f(M-\mu)-T]+\mu w;$$

$$I(\underline{\mathbf{P}})=\underline{p}[f(M-\mu)-T]+\mu w.$$

Proposition 12: With a real land tax T,
(i) if a household is risk-neutral, then the real land tax has no effect on rural-urban migration, i.e. $d\mu/dT=0$;
(ii) for any risk-averse household, when the real land tax increases, rural-urban migration will decrease, i.e. $d\mu/dT<0$.

Proof: see Appendix.

Proposition 12 shows that the effect of a real land tax on rural-urban migration depends on the degree of risk aversion. The larger the risk aversion, the stronger the effect of the tax on rural-urban migrantion. In fact, in China the most important tax in the rural areas is the real land tax. A heavy real land tax in China further reduces rural-urban migration.

Migration of Landless Rural Households

In the previous part of the paper, I have analyzed the cases where all of the rural households have cropland. Next, I extend this model to cases of landless rural households.

The migration problem for a landless household is the following:

$$\text{Max.} \quad qU(\mathbf{P}^*,p^**(M-\mu_L)f_r'(n_r+M-\mu_r)+\mu_L w)$$
$$\mu_L$$

$$+ (1-q)U(\underline{\mathbf{P}},\underline{p}(M-\mu_L)f_r'(n_r+M-\mu_r)+\mu_L w). \qquad (7^*)$$

$$\text{s.t.} \quad \mu_r = \text{argmax.} \ U^r$$

$$= qU(\mathbf{P}^*,p[f_r(n_r+M-\mu_r)-n_r f_r'(n_r+M-\mu_r)]$$

$$+ \mu_r w + (1-q)U(\underline{\mathbf{P}},\underline{p}[f_r(n_r+M-\mu_r)$$

$$- n_r f_r'(n_r+M-\mu_r)]+\mu_r w). \qquad (8)$$

Here, μ_L is the number of rural-urban migrants from a landless rural household.

(8) can be replaced by its FOC as follows:

$$qU_I(w-p^*f_r'(n_r+M-\mu_r)+n_r p^* f_r''(n_r+M-\mu_r))$$

$$+ (1-q)U_I(w-\underline{p}f_r'(n_r+M-\mu_r)+n_r\underline{p}f_r''(n_r+M-\mu_r))=0. \qquad (8a)$$

The FOC of problem (7^*) are the following:

$$\partial U/\partial \mu_L = qu_I(w-p^*f_r') + (1-q)U_I(w-\underline{p}f_r'). \qquad (10^*)$$

Here, f_r' is the marginal labor productivity of a rich household farm, and it is independent of μ_L.

In general, $\partial U/\partial \mu_L$ does not equal zero, i.e. there is no interior solution for the landless households. If the gap between the real urban wage and the agricultural income in a good state is wide and the landless rural households are optimistic about the state of nature, such that the expected marginal utility of migrating to the city is positive, i.e. $\partial U/\partial \mu_L > 0$, or $qu_I(w-p^*f_r') > (1-q)U_I(\underline{p}f_r'-w)$, then all of the landless laborers migrate to cities. Obviously, if the marginal labor productivity in agriculture is very low, then we must have $qu_I(w-p^*f_r') > (1-q)U_I(\underline{p}f_r'-w)$. However, if landless rural households are pessimistic about the state of nature, and agricultural income is significantly higher than the real urban wage in a bad state, such that the expected marginal utility of migrating to the city is negative, i.e. $\partial U/\partial \mu_L < 0$, or $qu_I(w-p^*f_r') < (1-q)U_I(\underline{p}f_r'-w)$, then none of the landless laborers migrate to cities; instead, they take agricultural jobs either by migrating to other rural areas or by renting cropland in their home villages. Similarly, if the marginal labor productivity in agriculture is quite high, say $f_r'=w/p^*$, then we must have $qu_I(w-p^*f_r') < (1-q)U_I(\underline{p}f_r'-w)$.

Proposition 13: For landless rural households,

(i) all landless rural household members migrate to cities if the marginal labor productivity in agriculture is very low, i.e. if $f_r' \rightarrow 0$;

(ii) all landless rural household members stay in agriculture if the marginal labor productivity in agriculture is high, i.e. if $f_r' \rightarrow w/p^*$.

These results provide some clues to explain the differences between the reformed Chinese economy and some other developing economies. In China and in other developing countries, rural housholds face a similar problem: the marginal labor productivity in agriculture is very low. However, in China, almost all of the rural households have land, and rural-urban migrants face big uncertainties in the free markets. According to the results above, under these conditions migration will be limited to a low level. In contrast, in most developing countries (similarly in the early stages of the British industrial revolution), considerable number of rural households are landless, and rural-urban migrants are not as clearly differentiated from other urban residents in the markets as they are in China. When the real urban wage is sufficiently higher than agricultural income in a good state, such that the expected marginal utility of migrating to the cities is positive, more landless people will migrate to the cities. "Too much" migration and migration-related unemployment may be the result.

CONCLUSION

This paper explains the following phenomena in rural areas observed during the period of reform in China: (i) compared with poor rural areas, more people in rich rural areas migrate to urban-suburban areas where wages are higher; (ii) people in poor rural areas migrate more to rich rural areas, where wages are higher than in poor rural areas but lower than in urban areas, than migrate to urban areas, while many rich rural area people migrate to urban areas. The theory is based on the nature of the risks faced by out-migrants and their families -- regarding rural households as geographically extended cooperative families.

In this theory, migration is regarded as an instrument of the income portfolio of a household: facing high risks of food price fluctuations of, a geographically extended cooperative household which has land and has out-migrants regards city jobs as high-risk high-income opportunities, and regards agricultural production on its own land as low-risk low-income opportunities. Agricultural production serves as an insurance for rural households. The "excess" labor input in agriculture and the resultant lower marginal labor productivity in agricultural production is virtually the payment for the insurance of the rural households.

Regarding migration as an instrument of the income portfolio of a household, if poorer households are more risk-averse than rich households, then a poor rural household will have a fewer number of rural-urban migrants than a richer rural household. An important implication of this result is that the poor become poorer and the rich become richer when there are opportunities for rural laborers to migrate to cities, and migration provides better chances to earn higher incomes.

Another implication of the theory is an explanation for the coexistence of low agricultural income and high city wages: it is due to the "excess" number of laborers in agriculture, which results from the rational choice of restricting the rural-urban migration from risk-averse rural households when there are uncertainties and the market is incomplete.

There are alternative plausible explanations for related questions. In the following, we show that these alternatives may not fit well with the central questions of this paper. The first one is the high cost of migration (e.g. transportation costs and adjustment costs). This explanation may be correct in some respects, but it does not help to explain the phenomenon that many people in poor rural areas migrate to rich rural areas instead of urban areas, while numerous people in rich rural areas migrate to cities.

The second explanation concerns the administrative restrictions on rural-urban migration. There were abundant harsh administrative restrictions on rural-urban migration before the reforms. However, after the reforms, most of the administrative restrictions were substantially loosened. For out-migration, in many circumastances administrative restrictions have been replaced by economic measures: fixed fees are charged to the people who wish to migrate. In fact, the fixed fees can simply be regarded as part of the migration costs.[16] Restrictions on immigration have also been loosened or even lifted.[17] Furthermore, administrative restrictions on immigration cannot explain the phenomenon that fewer poor rural laborers migrate to cities but more of them migrate to rich rural areas.

The third plausible explanation is based on the psychology of the rural populace: rural people do not enjoy an overcrowded city life, thus they prefer to stay in the countryside. However, in China the gap in the living standard between the cities and the countryside is great (the major source of income inequality in China is that between the city and the countryside). Therefore, most rural residents prefer to move to the cities if they are hired by a state owned-enterprise.[18]

APPENDIX

Proof of Proposition 1:

Problem (5) is strictly concave which can be shown by the following SOC:

$$d\Phi/d\mu = q[U_I(\mathbf{P}^*,Ip^*(^*f''+U_{II}(\mathbf{P}^*,I)(w-p^*f')^2]$$
$$+(1-q)[U_{II}(\mathbf{P}^*,I)(w-\underline{p}f')^2+U_I(\underline{\mathbf{P}},I)f'']$$
$$< 0. \qquad (7)$$

Here, $U_{II}(\mathbf{P}^*,I(\mathbf{P}^*))=\partial^2 U(\mathbf{P}^*,I(\mathbf{P}^*))/\partial I^2(\mathbf{P}^*)$ and $U_{II}(\underline{\mathbf{P}},I(\underline{\mathbf{P}}))=\partial^2 U(\underline{\mathbf{P}},I(\underline{\mathbf{P}}))/\partial I^2(\underline{\mathbf{P}})$. Moreover, μ is confined to a closed interval [0,m]. Therefore, problem (5) has a unique solution. ∎

Lemma 1: When all the parameters are fixed, (i) in the case of $\underline{p}_m=\beta p_m$, $\underline{p}=\beta p$, and w=const, the FOC (6) can be approximated in the neighborhood of the given parameters as follows:

$$\Phi \approx U_I(\mathbf{P}^*,(p^*/\underline{p})I(\underline{\mathbf{P}}))\{-r(\mathbf{P}^*,(p^*/\underline{p})I(\underline{\mathbf{P}}))q\mu w(1-p^*/\underline{p})$$
$$+[q(w-p^*f')+(1-q)(p^*/\underline{p})(w-\underline{p}f')]\}.$$

Here, r(.) is the ARA (absolute risk aversion) evaluated with given parameters;

(ii) in the case of $p_m = \underline{p}_m = 1$, the FOC (6) can be approximated in the neighborhood of the given parameters as follows:

$$\Phi \approx U_I(\underline{p}, I(\underline{p}))\{-r(\underline{p}, I(\underline{p}))q(w-p^*f')(\underline{p}-p)f$$
$$+[q(w-p^*f')+(1-q)(w-\underline{p}f')]\}+qU_{Ip}(\underline{p}, I(\underline{p}))[\underline{p}-p](w-p^*f').$$

Here, r(.) is the ARA (absolute risk aversion) evaluated with given parameters;

(iii) if $\underline{p}_m = \beta p_m$ and $\underline{p} = \beta p$, any interior solution μ^* must satisfy the following condition:

$$[w-p^*f'(M-\mu^*)]>[(1-q)/q](p^*/\underline{p})[\underline{p}f'(M-\mu^*)-w];$$

if $p_m = \underline{p}_m = 1$, any interior solution μ^* must satisfy the following condition:

$$(w-p^*f'(M-\mu^*))>[(1-q)/q](\underline{p}f'(M-\mu^*)-w);$$

(iv) if r(.) goes to infinity, there is no interior solution.

Proof of Lemma 1:
(i) $\underline{p}_m = \beta p_m$ and $\underline{p} = \beta p$ case. The indirect utility is homogeneous degree of zero[19], that is,

$U(\mathbf{P}^*,I) = U(\alpha\mathbf{P}^*,\alpha I)$ or $U_I(\mathbf{P}^*,I) = \alpha U_I(\alpha\mathbf{P}^*,\alpha I)$. Therefore, let $\beta = \underline{p}/p^*$,

$$
\begin{aligned}
U_I(\underline{\mathbf{P}},I(\underline{\mathbf{P}})) &= U_I(\beta p, \beta(1/\beta)I(\underline{\mathbf{P}})) \\
&= (1/\beta)U_I(\mathbf{P}^*,(1/\beta)I(\underline{\mathbf{P}})) \\
&= (p^*/\underline{p})U_I(\mathbf{P}^*,(p^*/\underline{p})I(\underline{\mathbf{P}})).
\end{aligned}
$$

Moreover, $(p^*/\underline{p})I(\underline{\mathbf{P}}) = p^*f + (p^*/\underline{p})\mu w < p^*f + \mu w = I(\mathbf{P}^*)$, $U(\mathbf{P}^*,I(\mathbf{P}^*))$ $>$ $U(\mathbf{P}^*,(p^*/\underline{p})I(\underline{\mathbf{P}}))$ for any $p < \underline{p}$. Thus, $U_I(\mathbf{P}^*,I(\mathbf{P}^*)) <$ $U_I(\mathbf{P}^*,(p^*/\underline{p})I(\underline{\mathbf{P}}))$. Given p, $\underline{p}$ and other parameters, $U_I(\mathbf{P}^*,I(\mathbf{P}^*))$ can be approximated in the neighborhood of $U_I(\mathbf{P}^*,(p^*/\underline{p})I(\underline{\mathbf{P}}))$:

$$
\begin{aligned}
U_I(\mathbf{P}^*,I(\mathbf{P}^*)) \quad &\approx U_I(\mathbf{P}^*,(p^*/\underline{p})I(\underline{\mathbf{P}})) \\
&\qquad + U_{II}(\mathbf{P}^*,(p^*/\underline{p})I(\underline{\mathbf{P}}))[I(\mathbf{P}^*)-(p^*/\underline{p})I(\underline{\mathbf{P}})] \\
&= U_I(\mathbf{P}^*,(p^*/\underline{p})I(\underline{\mathbf{P}})) \\
&\qquad + U_{II}(\mathbf{P}^*,(p^*/\underline{p})I(\underline{\mathbf{P}}))\mu w(1-p^*/\underline{p}).
\end{aligned}
$$

Using the above results to rearrange (6),

$$
\begin{aligned}
\Phi &= qU_I(\mathbf{P}^*,I(\mathbf{P}^*))(w-p^*f') + (1-q)U_I(\underline{\mathbf{P}},I(\underline{\mathbf{P}}))(w-\underline{p}f') \\
&= q[U_I(\mathbf{P}^*,I(\mathbf{P}^*)) - (\underline{p}/p^*)U_I(\underline{\mathbf{P}},I(\underline{\mathbf{P}}))](w-p^*f') \\
&\qquad + U_I(\underline{\mathbf{P}},I(\underline{\mathbf{P}}))[q(\underline{p}/p^*)(w-p^*f') + (1-q)(w-\underline{p}f')] \\
&= q[U_I(\mathbf{P}^*,I(\mathbf{P}^*)) - U_I(\mathbf{P}^*,(p^*/\underline{p})I(\underline{\mathbf{P}}))](w-p^*f') \\
&\qquad + U_I(\mathbf{P}^*,(p^*/\underline{p})I(\underline{p}))[q(w-p^*f') + (1-q)(p^*/\underline{p})(w-\underline{p}f')] \\
&\approx qU_{II}(\mathbf{P}^*,(p^*/\underline{p})I(\underline{\mathbf{P}}))[I(\mathbf{P}^*)-(p^*/\underline{p})I(\underline{\mathbf{P}})](w-p^*f') \\
&\qquad + U_I(\mathbf{P}^*,(p^*/\underline{p})I(\underline{\mathbf{P}}))[q(w-p^*f') + (1-q)(p^*/\underline{p})(w-\underline{p}f')] \\
&= U_I(\mathbf{P}^*,(p^*/\underline{p})I(\underline{\mathbf{P}}))\{-r(\mathbf{P}^*,(p^*/\underline{p})I(\underline{\mathbf{P}}))q\mu w(1-p^*/\underline{p}) \\
&\qquad + [q(w-p^*f') + (1-q)(p^*/\underline{p})(w-\underline{p}f')]\}. \qquad (6')
\end{aligned}
$$

Here, $r(\mathbf{P}^*,(p^*/\underline{p})I(\underline{\mathbf{P}})) = -U_{II}(\mathbf{P}^*,(p^*/\underline{p})I(\underline{\mathbf{P}}))/U_I(\mathbf{P}^*,(p^*/\underline{p})I(\underline{\mathbf{P}}))$ is the ARA evaluated with the given parameters. Assuming that all parameters are fixed, then $r(.)$ can be treated as a parameter r.

(ii) $p_m=\underline{p}_m=1$ case. Given p, $\underline{p}$ and other parameters, $U_I(p,I(p))$ can be approximated in the neighbor of $U_I(\underline{p},I(\underline{p}))$:

$$U_I(p,I(p)) \approx U_I(\underline{p},I(\underline{p}))+U_{II}(\underline{p},I(\underline{p}))[I(\underline{p})$$
$$-I(p)]+U_{Ip}(\underline{p},I(\underline{p}))[\underline{p}-p]$$
$$= U_I(\underline{p},I(\underline{p}))+U_{II}(\underline{p},I(\underline{p}))(\underline{p}-p)f$$
$$+U_{Ip}(\underline{p},I(\underline{p}))[\underline{p}-p].$$

Using the above results to rearrange (6),

$$\Phi= qU_I(p,I(p))(w-p^*f')+(1-q)U_I(\underline{p},I(\underline{p}))(w-\underline{p}f')$$
$$= q[U_I(p,I(p))-U_I(\underline{p},I(\underline{p}))](w-p^*f')$$
$$+U_I(\underline{p},I(\underline{p}))[q(w-p^*f')+(1-q)(w-\underline{p}f')]$$
$$\approx q\{U_{II}(\underline{p},I(\underline{p}))[I(\underline{p})-I(p)]+U_{Ip}(\underline{p},I(\underline{p}))[\underline{p}-p]\}(w-p^*f')$$
$$+U_I(\underline{p},I(\underline{p}))[q(w-p^*f')+(1-q)(w-\underline{p}f')]$$
$$= U_I(\underline{p},I(\underline{p}))\{-r(\underline{p},I(\underline{p}))q(w-p^*f')(\underline{p}-p)f$$
$$+[q(w-p^*f')+(1-q)(w-\underline{p}f')]\}$$
$$+qU_{Ip}(\underline{p},I(\underline{p}))[\underline{p}-p](w-p^*f'). \qquad (6'')$$

Here, $r(\underline{p},I(\underline{p})) = -U_{II}(\underline{p},I(\underline{p}))/U_I(\underline{p},I(\underline{p}))$ is the ARA evaluated with the given parameters. Assuming that all parameters are fixed, then $r(.)$ can be treated as a parameter r.

(iii)   From (6'),

$\Phi \approx U_I(\mathbf{P}^*,(p^*/\underline{p})I(\underline{\mathbf{P}}))\{-r(\mathbf{P}^*,(p^*/\underline{p})I(\underline{\mathbf{P}}))q\mu w(1-p^*/\underline{p})+[q(w-p^*f')$
$+(1-q)(p^*/\underline{p})(w-\underline{p}f')]\}=0.$

This implies $q(w-p^*f')+(1-q)(p^*/\underline{p})(w-\underline{p}f')>0$ or
$[w-p^*f']>[(1-q)/q][\underline{p}f'-w].$
From (6"),

$\Phi \approx U_I(\underline{p},I(\underline{p}))\{-r(\underline{p},I(\underline{p}))q(w-p^*f')(\underline{p}-p)f$
$\qquad +[q(w-p^*f')+(1-q)(w-\underline{p}f')]\}$
$\qquad +qU_{Ip}(\underline{p},I(\underline{p}))[\underline{p}-p](w-p^*f')$
$= 0.$

This implies $q(w-p^*f')+(1-q)(w-\underline{p}f')>0$, or
$(w-p^*f')>[(1-q)/q](\underline{p}f'-w).$

(iv) It is obvious from (6') and (6"). ∎

Proof of Proposition 1:
(i) $\underline{p}_m=\beta p_m$ and $\underline{p}=\beta p$ case. If $r(.) = 0$, by Lemma 1, (6') is reduced to the following:

$$\Phi = U_I(\underline{\mathbf{P}},I(\underline{\mathbf{P}}))[w-f'(qp+(1-q)\underline{p}] = 0.$$
Or,
$$qw+(1-q)w = qp^*f'+(1-q)\underline{p}f'.$$

This simply means:
    Expected real city wage = Expected agricultural marginal income.

(ii) $p_m = \underline{p}_m = 1$ case. If $r(.) = 0$, by Lemma 1, (6") is reduced to the following:

$$\Phi \approx U_I(\underline{p}, I(\underline{p}))[q(w-p^*f')+(1-q)(w-\underline{p}f')]$$
$$+qU_{Ip}(\underline{p}, I(\underline{p}))[\underline{p}-p](w-p^*f')$$
$$= 0.$$

Since $qU_{Ip}(\underline{p}, I(\underline{p}))[\underline{p}-p](w-p^*f')<0$, this implies

$$q(w-p^*f')+(1-q)(w-\underline{p}f')>0,$$

or

$$qw+(1-q)w > qp^*f'+(1-q)\underline{p}f'.$$

(iii) By Lemma 1, $d\Phi/dr = -U_I(P^*,(p^*/\underline{p})I(\underline{P}))q\mu w(1-p^*/\underline{p})<0$.
          $d\mu/dr = -\Phi_r/\Phi_\mu < 0.$ ■

Proof of Proposition 3:

(i) By (6), $\Phi = qU_I(P^*,I(P^*))(w-p^*f')+(1-q)U_I(\underline{P},I(\underline{P}))(w-\underline{p}f')$. Thus,

$$\Phi_q = U_I(P^*,I(P^*))(w-p^*f')-U_I(\underline{P},I(\underline{P}))(w-\underline{p}f').$$

By assumptions (a) and (b),

          $\Phi_q>0$, or $d\mu/dq>0$.

(ii) Similarly,
$\Phi_p = q[U_{Ip}(P^*,I(P^*))(w-p^*f')-U_I(P^*,I(P^*))f'$
$+U_{II}(P^*,I(P^*))(w-p^*f')f]<0,$
i.e. $d\mu/dp<0$.

(iii) $\Phi_{\underline{p}} = (1-q)[U_{Ip}(\underline{P},I(\underline{P}))-U_I(\underline{P},I(\underline{P}))f'+U_{II}(\underline{P},I(\underline{P}))(w-\underline{p}f')f]$

$$=(1-q)\{U_{I\underline{p}}(\underline{P},I(\underline{P}))-U_I(\underline{P},I(\underline{P}))[f'+r(\underline{P},I(\underline{P}))(w-\underline{p}f')f]\}$$

$$\lim_{r\to 0}\phi_{\underline{p}} \text{ i.e. } \lim_{r\to 0}\frac{d\mu}{d\underline{p}}<0$$

Proof of Proposition 4:

$$\Phi=qU_I(\mathbf{P}^*,I(\mathbf{P}^*))(w-p^*f')+(1-q)U_I(\underline{P},I(\underline{P}))(w-\underline{p}f')$$
$$\Phi_w=q[U_I(\mathbf{P}^*,I(\mathbf{P}^*))+U_{II}(\mathbf{P}^*,I(\mathbf{P}^*))(w-p^*f')\mu]$$
$$+(1-q)[U_I(\underline{P},I(\underline{P}))+U_{II}(\underline{P},I(\underline{P}))(w-\underline{p}f')\mu]$$
$$=qU_I(\mathbf{P}^*,I(\mathbf{P}^*))[1-r(\mathbf{P}^*,I(\mathbf{P}^*))(w-p^*f')\mu]$$
$$+(1-q)U_I(\underline{P},I(\underline{P}))[1-r(\underline{P},I(\underline{P}))(w-\underline{p}f')\mu]$$

(iii) In general, for $r(.)>0$, sign Φ_w is ambiguous. Thus, $d\mu/dw$ is indeterminate.

(i) $\lim_{r\to 0}\phi_w = qU_I(\mathbf{P}^*,I(\mathbf{P}^*))+(1-q)U_I(\underline{P},I(\underline{P})) > 0.$

(ii) $\lim_{\mu\to 0}\phi_w = qU_I(\mathbf{P}^*,I(\mathbf{P}^*))+(1-q)U_I(\underline{P},I(\underline{P})) > 0.$ ∎

Proof of Proposition 5:

$$\Phi_m=q[U_I(\mathbf{P}^*,I)(-p^*f'')+U_{II}(\mathbf{P}^*,Ip^*(^*f'(w-p^*f')]$$
$$+(1-q)[U_I(\underline{P},I)(-\underline{p}f'')+U_{II}(\underline{P},I)(w-\underline{p}f')\underline{p}f']$$
$$=qU_I(\mathbf{P}^*,I)[-p^*f''-r(\mathbf{P}^*,I)p^*f'(w-p^*f')]$$
$$+(1-q)U_I(\underline{P},I)[-\underline{p}f''-r(\underline{P},I)(w-\underline{p}f')\underline{p}f'].$$

(iii) In general, when $r(.)>0$, sign Φ_m is ambiguous.

(i) $\lim_{r \to 0} \phi_m = qU_I(\mathbf{P^*},I)[-p^*f''] + (1-q)U_I(\underline{\mathbf{P}},I)[-\underline{p}f''] > 0.$

(ii) $\lim_{f' \to 0} \phi_m = qU_I(\mathbf{P^*},I)[-p^*f''] + (1-q)U_I(\underline{\mathbf{P}},I)[-\underline{p}f''] > 0.$ ∎

Proof of Proposition 6:

Problem (7) is strictly concave which can be shown by the following SOCs:

$U_{nn} = qp[U_{II}(f_r'(n_r+M-\mu_r)-f_p'(M-n-\mu_p))^2 + U_I f_p''(M-n-\mu_p)]$
$\qquad + (1-q)\underline{p}[U_{II}(f_r'(n_r+M-\mu_r)-f_p'(M-n-\mu_p))^2 + U_I f_p''(M-n-\mu_p)]$
$\quad = qpU_I[-r(.)(f_r'(n_r+M-\mu_r)-f_p'(M-n-\mu_p))^2 + f_p''(M-n-\mu_p)]$
$\qquad + (1-q)\underline{p}U_I[-r(.)(f_r'(n_r+M-\mu_r)-f_p'(M-n-\mu_p))^2$
$\qquad + f_p''(M-n-\mu_p)]$
$\quad = [qpU_I(\mathbf{P^*},I_p(\mathbf{P^*})) + (1-q)\underline{p}(U_I(\underline{\mathbf{P}},I_p(\underline{\mathbf{P}}))]\, f_p''(M-n-\mu_p)$

< 0 \hfill (11)

From (9),

$U_{n\mu} = qp[U_{II}(f_r'(n_r+M-\mu_r)-f_p'(M-n-\mu_p))(w-p^*f_p') + U_I f_p''(M-n-\mu_p)]$
$\qquad + (1-q)\underline{p}[U_{II}(f_r'(n+M-\mu_r)$
$\qquad - f_p'(M-n-\mu_p))(w-\underline{p}f_p') + U_I f_p''(M-n-\mu_p))]$
$\quad = qpU_I[-r(.)(f_r'(n+M-\mu_r)-f_p'(M-n-\mu_p))(w-p^*f_p') + f_p''(M-n-\mu_p)]$

$$+ (1-q)\underline{p}U_I[-r(.)(f_r'(n+M-\mu_r)$$
$$- f_p'(M-n-\mu_p))(w-\underline{p}f_p')+f_p''(M-n-\mu_p))]$$
$$= qpU_I(\mathbf{P}^*,I_p(\mathbf{P}^*)) + (1-q)\underline{p}U_I(\underline{\mathbf{P}},I_p(\underline{\mathbf{P}}))]f_p''(M-n-\mu_p))$$
$$< 0 \tag{12}$$

From (10),

$$U_{\mu\mu}= q[U_{II}(w-p^*f_p')^2 + U_I(p^*f_p'')] + (1-q)[U_{II}(w-\underline{p}f_p')^2+U_I(\underline{p}f_p'')]$$
$$= qU_I[-r(.)(w-p^*f_p')^2 + (p^*f_p'')]$$
$$+ (1-q)U_I[-r(.)(w-\underline{p}f_p')^2+(\underline{p}f_p'')]$$
$$< 0 \tag{13}$$

$$|J| = \begin{vmatrix} U_{nn} & U_{n\mu} \\ U_{n\mu} & U_{\mu\mu} \end{vmatrix}$$

$$= U_{nn}U_{\mu\mu} - U_{n\mu}^2$$
$$= [qpU_I(g) + (1-q)\underline{p}(U_I(b)] f_p''(M-n-\mu_p)\{qU_I(g)[-r(.)(w-p^*f_p')^2 +$$
$$(p^*f_p'')] + (1-q)U_I(b)[-r(.)(w-\underline{p}f_p')^2+(\underline{p}f_p'')]\}$$
$$- [qpU_I(g) + (1-q)\underline{p}U_I(b)]^2 [f_p''(M-n-\mu_p))]^2$$
$$= [qpU_I(g) + (1-q)\underline{p}U_I(b)] f_p'' [qU_I(gp^*(^*f_p'' + (1-q)U_I(b)\underline{p}f_p'']$$
$$- [qpU_I(g) + (1-q)\underline{p}U_I(b)]^2 [f_p'']^2$$
$$+ [qpU_I(g)+(1-q)\underline{p}U_I(b)] f_p'' [qU_I(g)r(.)(w-p^*f_p')^2$$
$$+(1-q)U_I(b)r(.)(w-\underline{p}f_p')^2]$$
$$= [qpU_I(g) + (1-q)\underline{p}U_I(b)]^2 f_p'' f_p''$$
$$- [qpU_I(g) + (1-q)\underline{p}U_I(b)]^2 [f_p'']^2$$
$$+ [qpU_I(g)+(1-q)\underline{p}U_I(b)] f_p'' [qU_I(g)r(.)(w-p^*f_p')^2$$
$$+ (1-q)U_I(b)r(.)(w-\underline{p}f_p')^2]$$

$$= qpU_I(g)+(1-q)\underline{p}(U_I(b)] \ f_p" \ [qU_I(g)r(.)(w-p^*f_p')^2$$
$$+ (1-q)U_I(b)r(.)(w-\underline{p}f_p')^2$$
$$> 0 \hspace{6cm} (14)$$

Moreover, both μ_p and n are confined to a closed interval [0,m]. Therefore, problem (7) has an unique maximum.■

Proof of Proposition 7:

The FOC (10) is the same as (6). Therefore, Lemma 1 is applicable to problem (7). By Lemma 1(i),

$$U_\mu \quad \approx U_I(\mathbf{P}^*,(p^*/\underline{p})I(\underline{\mathbf{P}}))\{-r(\mathbf{P}^*,(p^*/\underline{p})I(\underline{\mathbf{P}}))q\mu w(1-p^*/\underline{p})$$
$$+ [q(w-p^*f')+(1-q)(p^*/\underline{p})(w-\underline{p}f')] \hspace{2cm} (10')$$

Here, $r(\mathbf{P}^*,(p^*/\underline{p})I(\underline{\mathbf{P}})) = -U_{II}(\mathbf{P}^*,(p^*/\underline{p})I(\underline{\mathbf{P}}))/U_I(\mathbf{P}^*,(p^*/\underline{p})I(\underline{\mathbf{P}}))$ is the ARA evaluated with the given parameters. Assuming that all parameters are fixed, r(.) can be treated as a parameter.
(i) When r(.)=0,

$$U_\mu \quad \approx U_I(\mathbf{P}^*,(p^*/\underline{p})I(\underline{\mathbf{P}}))[q(w-p^*f')$$
$$+ (1-q)(p^*/\underline{p})(w-\underline{p}f')] \hspace{3cm} (10")$$

At equilibrium, when r(.)=0, n^* and μ_p^* are chosen such that (10") and (9') are satisfied. (10") implies that

$$qw+(1-q)w = qp^*f_p'(M-n^*-\mu_p^*)+(1-q)\underline{p}f_p'(M-n^*-\mu_p^*).$$

To prove the remaining part of the proposition, totally

differentiate the FOCs (9) and (10):

$$U_{nn}dn + U_{n\mu}d\mu_p = - U_{np}dp - U_{n\underline{p}}d\underline{p} - U_{nq}dq$$
$$- U_{nm}dm - U_{nw}dw - U_{nr}dr \qquad (15)$$

$$U_{\mu n}dn + U_{\mu\mu}d\mu_p = - U_{\mu p}dp - U_{\mu\underline{p}}d\underline{p} - U_{\mu q}dq$$
$$- U_{\mu m}dm - U_{\mu w}dw - U_{\mu r}dr \qquad (16)$$

Rearrange (15) and (16),

$$\begin{bmatrix} U_{nn} & U_{n\mu} \\ U_{\mu n} & U_{\mu\mu} \end{bmatrix} \begin{bmatrix} \partial n/\partial r \\ \partial \mu_p/\partial r \end{bmatrix} = \begin{bmatrix} -U_{nr} \\ -U_{\mu r} \end{bmatrix} = \begin{bmatrix} 0 \\ U_I(\underline{P},I(\underline{P}))q(\underline{p}-p)f_p{'}(w-p^*f_p{'})>0 \end{bmatrix}.$$

$$\frac{\partial n}{\partial r} = \frac{\begin{vmatrix} -U_{nr} & U_{n\mu} \\ -U_{\mu r} & U_{\mu\mu} \end{vmatrix}}{|J|}$$

$$\frac{\partial \mu_p}{\partial r} = \frac{\begin{vmatrix} U_{nn} & -U_{nr} \\ U_{\mu n} & -U_{\mu r} \end{vmatrix}}{|J|}$$

Since $|J|>0$,

$$\text{sign } \partial n/\partial r = U_{n\mu}U_{\mu r}, \qquad (17)$$

and

$$\text{sign } \partial \mu_p/\partial r = -U_{nn}U_{\mu r}. \qquad (18)$$

Differentiate (10') with respect to r,

$$U_{\mu r} = -U_I(\mathbf{P}^*, (p^*/\underline{p})I(\underline{\mathbf{P}}))q\mu w(1-p^*/\underline{p}) < 0. \tag{19}$$

(ii) By (18), (19) and (11), sign $\partial\mu_p/\partial r = -U_{nn}U_{\mu r} = U_{nn} < 0$.

(iii) By (17), (19) and (12), sign $\partial n/\partial r = U_{n\mu}U_{\mu r} > 0$.

(iv) Given $r_p > r_r$, $\partial\mu_p/\partial r < 0$ and $\partial\mu_r/\partial r < 0$, $\mu_r > \mu_p$.

(v) Given $m_r = m_p = m$ and $\mu_r > \mu_p$, the result is obvious. ∎

Proof of Proposition 8:
(i) Rearrange (15) and (16),

$$\begin{bmatrix} U_{nn} & U_{n\mu} \\ U_{\mu n} & U_{\mu\mu} \end{bmatrix} \begin{bmatrix} \partial n/\partial p \\ \partial\mu_p/\partial p \end{bmatrix} = \begin{bmatrix} -U_{nb} \\ -U_{\mu p} \end{bmatrix} = \begin{bmatrix} 0 \\ qU_I wf_p' > 0 \end{bmatrix}.$$

$$\frac{\partial n}{\partial p} = \frac{\begin{vmatrix} -U_{np} & U_{n\mu} \\ -U_{\mu p} & U_{\mu\mu} \end{vmatrix}}{|J|}$$

$$\frac{\partial\mu_p}{\partial p} = \frac{\begin{vmatrix} U_{nn} & -U_{np} \\ U_{\mu n} & -U_{\mu p} \end{vmatrix}}{|J|}$$

Since $|J|>0$,

$\text{sign } (\partial\mu_p/\partial p) = U_{nn} < 0$

$\text{sign } (\partial n/\partial p) = -U_{n\mu} > 0.$

(ii) and (iii) Similarly,

$U_{np}=0$ and $-U_{\mu\underline{p}}=(1-q)U_If_p'>0$. Thus,

$\text{sign } (\partial n/\partial \underline{p}) = -U_{n\mu} > 0$ and

$\text{sign } (\partial\mu_p/\partial \underline{p}) = U_{nn} < 0.$

$U_{nq}=0$ and $-U_{\mu q}=-(U_I(w-p^*f_p') - U_I(w-\underline{p}f_p'))<0$. Thus,

$\text{sign } (\partial n/\partial q) = U_{n\mu} < 0$ and

$\text{sign } (\partial\mu_p/\partial q) = -U_{nn} > 0.$ ∎

Proof of Proposition 9:

Let us proof part (iii) first. By (9), (10), (15) and (16),

(20)
$$\frac{\partial n}{\partial w} = \frac{\begin{vmatrix} -U_{nw} & U_{n\mu} \\ -U_{\mu w} & U_{\mu\mu} \end{vmatrix}}{|J|}$$

(21)
$$\frac{\partial \mu_p}{\partial w} = \frac{\begin{vmatrix} U_{nn} & -U_{nw} \\ U_{\mu n} & -U_{\mu w} \end{vmatrix}}{|J|}$$

$U_{nw} = 0.$

$$-U_{\mu w} = -\{q[U_{II}(g)(w-p^*f_p')\mu_p + U_I(g)]$$
$$+ (1-q)[U_{II}(b)(w-\underline{p}f_p')\mu_p + U_I(b)\}$$
$$= qU_I(g)[r(g)(w-p^*f_p')\mu_p - 1]$$
$$+ (1-q)U_I(b)[r(b)(w-\underline{p}f_p')\mu_p - 1]$$

(iii) In general, sign $(-U_{\mu w})$ is ambiguous. By (20) and (21),

$$\text{sign } \partial n/\partial w = \text{sign } U_{n\mu}U_{\mu w} = \text{sign } -U_{\mu w} \text{ and}$$
$$\text{sign } \partial\mu_p/\partial w = \text{sign } -U_{nn}U_{\mu w} = \text{sign } U_{\mu w}.$$

Therefore, sign $\partial n/\partial w$ and sign $\partial\mu_p/\partial w = $sign $-dn/dw$ are ambiguous.

(i) $\lim\limits_{r \to 0} U_{\mu w} < 0.$

$$sign \; \{\lim\limits_{r \to 0} \frac{\partial n}{\partial w}\} = \text{sign } U_{n\mu} < 0$$

$$sign \; \{\lim\limits_{r \to 0} \frac{\partial\mu_p}{\partial w}\} (\frac{\mu p_p}{\mu_w}) = \text{sign } -U_{nn} > 0.$$

(ii) $\lim\limits_{\mu_p \to 0} -U_{\mu w} < 0.$

$$sign\{\lim\limits_{\mu_p \to 0} \frac{\partial n}{\partial w}\} = \text{sign } U_{n\mu} < 0$$

$$sign\{\lim_{\mu_p \to 0} \frac{\partial\mu_p}{\partial w}\} \, (\frac{\partial\mu_p}{\partial w}) \quad sign \, -U_{nn} > 0. \blacksquare$$

Proof of Proposition 10:

Let us proof part (iii) first. Rearrange (15) and (16),

$$\frac{\partial n}{\partial M} = \frac{\begin{vmatrix} -U_{nm} & U_{n\mu} \\ -U_{\mu m} & U_{\mu\mu} \end{vmatrix}}{|J|}$$

$$\frac{\partial \mu}{\partial m} = \frac{\begin{vmatrix} U_{nn} & -U_{nm} \\ U_{\mu m} & -U_{\mu m} \end{vmatrix}}{|J|}$$

sign $\partial n/\partial m$ = sign $(-U_{nm}U_{\mu\mu} + U_{n\mu}U_{\mu m})$, and

sign $\partial\mu_p/\partial m$ = sign $(-U_{nn}U_{\mu m} + U_{nm}U_{\mu n})$.

Here, sign $U_{nm} = f_r'' - f_p'' \leq 0$, if $f_r'' \leq f_p''$; $U_{nm} > 0$, otherwise.

$U_{\mu m} = qp[U_{II}(w - p^*f_p')f_p' - U_I f_p''] + (1-q)\underline{p}[U_{II}(w - \underline{p}f_p')f_p' - U_I f_p'']$

$\qquad = qpU_I[-r(g)(w - p^*f_p')f_p' - f_p''] + (1-q)\underline{p}U_I[-r(b)(w - \underline{p}f_p')f_p' - f_p'']$

(iii) In general, when $r(.) > 0$, sign $U_{\mu m}$ is ambiguous.

(i) $\lim\limits_{r \to 0} U_{\mu m} > 0$

If $f_r'' \leq f_p''$,

$$sign \; \{ \lim\limits_{r \to 0} sign \; \frac{\partial n}{\partial m} \} < 0, \quad and \quad \{ \lim\limits_{r \to 0} sign \; \frac{\partial \mu_p}{\partial m} \} > 0.$$

(ii) $\lim\limits_{f_p' \to 0} U_{\mu m} > 0$

If $f_r'' \leq f_p''$,

$$sign \; \{ \lim\limits_{f_p' \to 0} sign \; \frac{\partial n}{\partial m} \} < 0, \quad and \quad sign \; \{ \lim\limits_{f_p' \to 0} sign \; \frac{\partial \mu}{\partial m} \} > 0.$$

Proof of Proposition 11:

$\Phi_t = -qU_{II}(\mathbf{P^*},I(\mathbf{P^*}))(w-p^*f') - (1-q)U_{II}(\underline{\mathbf{P}},I(\underline{\mathbf{P}}))(w-\underline{p}f')$

$\quad = qU_I(\mathbf{P^*},I(\mathbf{P^*}))r(\mathbf{P^*},I(\mathbf{P^*}))(w-p^*f')$

$\qquad\qquad + (1-q)U_I(\underline{\mathbf{P}},I(\underline{\mathbf{P}}))r(\underline{\mathbf{P}},I(\underline{\mathbf{P}}))(w-\underline{p}f')$

(i) If $r(\mathbf{P^*},I(\mathbf{P^*})) = r(\underline{\mathbf{P}},I(\underline{\mathbf{P}})) = r$, by the FOC,

$\Phi_t = [qU_I(\mathbf{P^*},I(\mathbf{P^*}))(w-p^*f') + (1-q)U_I(\underline{\mathbf{P}},I(\underline{\mathbf{P}}))(w-\underline{p}f')]r = 0,$ i.e.
$d\mu/dt = 0$.

(ii) If $r(\mathbf{P^*},I(\mathbf{P^*})) < r(\underline{\mathbf{P}},I(\underline{\mathbf{P}}))$, by the FOC and assumptions (a) and
(b), $d\mu/dt < 0$.■

Proof of Proposition 12:

$$\Phi_T = qU_{II}(\mathbf{P}^*,I(\mathbf{P}^*))(w-p^*f')p^* - (1-q)U_{II}(\underline{\mathbf{P}},I(\underline{\mathbf{P}}))(w-\underline{p}f')\underline{p}$$
$$= qU_I(\mathbf{P}^*,I(\mathbf{P}^*))[r(\mathbf{P}^*,I(\mathbf{P}^*)p^*](w-p^*f')$$
$$+ (1-q)U_I(\underline{\mathbf{P}},I(\underline{\mathbf{P}}))[r(\underline{\mathbf{P}},I(\underline{\mathbf{P}}))\underline{p}](w-\underline{p}f')$$

(i) If r(.)=0, Φ_T=0, i.e. dμ/dT=0.

(ii) For any risk-averse household, since p<$\underline{p}$ and r($\mathbf{P}^*$)$\leq$r($\underline{\mathbf{P}}$), thus pr($\mathbf{P}^*$,I($\mathbf{P}^*$))=A<$\underline{pr}$($\underline{\mathbf{P}}$,I($\underline{\mathbf{P}}$))=B. By the FOC and assumptions (a) and (b),

$$\Phi_T = qU_I(\mathbf{P}^*,I(\mathbf{P}^*))(w-p^*f')A + (1-q)U_I(\underline{\mathbf{P}},I(\underline{\mathbf{P}}))(w-\underline{p}f')B < 0.$$

Therefore, dμ/dT<0.∎

ENDNOTES

1. In this paper I refer to all the areas where rural industry is concentrated as urban-suburban areas. In fact, about 70 percent of rural industrial enterprises are located in officially defined suburban areas (Perkins, 1987). Rural industry here is an official definition of industries run by rural residents. Actually, so-called rural industry includes the electronics, machine-building and mining industries etc. Moreover, more than one quarter of rural laborers are full-time workers in rural industrial enterprises.

2. However, evidence shows that the nominal urban wage in developing countries is usually 50-100 percent higher than nominal agricultural wage, and the unemployment rate is often lower than 10 percent, i.e. the expected urban wage is higher than the expected rural wage (Rowsenzweig, 1988, p.748).

3. To better investigate rural households' rural-urban and rural-rural migration behavior, I have eliminated the data from Shanghai which is a large city in the sample. Moreover, unfortunately, the only data available to the public is the aggregated data which has only ten independent observations. Therefore, a rigorous econometric study based on the data available is not feasible.

4. With an extremely limited supply of other foodstuffs, grain is the major source of calories for the Chinese. In fact, a serious shortage of grain results in famine in China.

5. Township village enterprises (TVE) are non-agricultural enterprises run by officially defined rural residents. In fact, over 70 percent of the TVEs are located in urban-suburban areas. The officially defined rural resident has nothing to do with the location where he/she works and also has nothing to do with the nature of his/her job. Rural residents are restricted by the grain supply -- they are not eligible to buy grain in the state stores.

6. To simplify the model, I assume away the random shock in agricultural production. It is easy to show that with the random shock in agricultural production in the model, the results of the model would not be changed provided that agricultural production is less risky than the city wages.

7. The Chinese government has set ceiling wages for all firms regardless of whether they are state-owned enterprises or TVEs to control the wage race, which is an important phenomenon in reformed Chinese economy. The wage race here refers to the fact that state-owned firms raise their wages to match higher standards of wages observed in other firms. When this race is prevailing, there will be run-away wage increases and run-away inflation. Further explanation on the wage-race is beyond the scope of this paper.
Evidence does suggests that ceilings on wages are binding: (i) TVE wages are not correlated to the marginal labor productivities; (ii) they are correlated with nearby state-owned enterprise wages (Xu, 1991).

8. When the ceiling wage is binding both in the good state and in the bad state, and the government does not change the ceiling wage in a bad state, the wage remains constant in both states.

9. Compared with urban occupasions, an opinion survey shows that most rural residents regarded farming as the worst occupation in the society in terms of income (IESR, 1988). Interpreting the good state in the model as a normal year, using rural incomes to approximate the marginal products of labor of agriculture, it is easy to find evidence that rural nominal incomes are significantly lower than urban nominal wages. For example, in 1988, average Chinese rural per capita annual income was 545 yuan, average Chinese urban per capita annual income was 1192 yuan (SSB, 1989, pp. 729-743). Suppose rural-urban migrants' annual income is the same as urban residence, in a normal year, if the food price in the free markets is 200 percent of the official price, and two third of migrants' expenditure is for food consumption, then the real income of rural-urban migrants is still higher than rural laborers.

10. Even in a normal year, food consumption accounted for more than half of the total consumptions for both rural and urban residents in China. In a bad state, when the price of food in the free markets increases greatly (e.g. in the early 1960s the food price increased several hundred percent in the free markets), the real income of rural-urban migrants, who rely completely on the free markets for food consumption, can be significantly lower than that of rural laborers, since rural laborers food consumption largely depends on their own agricultural products. According to official sample surveys, from 1978 to 1988, by average about two thirds of rural households' food consumption was made up of their own products (SSB, 1989, p.744). For urban resident households, who enjoy government subsidies and de facto insurance in food supplies, the share of food consumption was larger than 50 percent (SSB, 1989, pp.727-733). For rural-urban immigrants their share of the food consumption in their total expenditure must be significantly larger.

11. Here, only rural-urban migration is analyzed. The possibility of migration from a poor area to a rich area will be discussed later.

12. This is the basic assumption in the classical theory of dual economies (Lewis, 1954 and Ranis and Fei, 1961).

13. To focus on my point, I ignore the uncertainties in agricultural production and the contractual problems between a rich household, which hires laborers and provides land and capital, and employees. I simply assume that an employee earns his marginal product of labor.

14. If city firm managers are risk averse, wages will not be indexed. When the managers are also rural migrants, or when the firms are small, assuming managers risk aversion is easily justifiable.

15. The effect of many other lump sum taxes on rural-urban migration are virtually the same as the land taxes analyzed here.

16. The fee is usually lower than transportation costs and adjustment costs.

17. In 1988, the Chinese government officially lifted administrative restrictions on rural-urban immigration as long as migrants were able to provide their own food in cities (Forbes and Linge, 1990).

18. In an opinion survey conducted in 1985, most rural residents regarded farming as the worst occupation in the society in terms of income, and all the subjects regarded farming as the worst occupation in the society in terms of social status. Among the ten occupations which they were asked to compare with in the sample survey, all occupations except farming are concentrated in urban areas

(IESR, 1988).

19. To avoid the complications caused by $\partial^2 U/\partial I \partial p$, in the following the homogeneous property of the indirect utility function is employed.

REFERENCES

Alchian, Armen A., "Foreword," in Furubotn, Erik G., and Pejovich, Svetozar, *The Economics of Property Rights*, p.xiii, Cambridge (Mass.): Ballinger Publishing Company, 1974.

Alchian, Armen A. and Demsetz, Harold, "Production, Information Costs, and Economic Organization," *American Economic Review*, **62**, 5:777-795, December, 1972

American Rural Small-scale Industry Delegation, (1977), *Rural Small-Scale Industry in the People's Republic of China*. Berkeley: University of California Press.

Bergson, A., and H.Levine (eds.) (1983), *The Soviet Economy Towards the Year 2000*. London. Chapter 2.

Bliss, C., and Stern, N., (1978), "Productivity, Wages

and Nutrituion," Parts I and II, *Journal of Development Economics*, 5:331-398.

Byrd, William, and Lin Qingsong (eds.) (1990), *China's Rural Industry: Structure, Development, and Reform*. New York: Oxford University Press.

Chen, K., G.Jefferson, T.Rawski, H.Wang, and Y.Zheng, (1988), "Productivity Change in Chinese Industry: 1953-1985," *Journal of Comparative Economics*, 12:570-591.

Byrd, William A., "Entreprenership, Capital, and Ownership," in Byrd, William A.. and Lin, Qingsong (eds.), *China's Rural Industry: Structure, Development and Reform*, pp.189-218. New York: Oxford University Press, 1990.

Byrd, William A., and Lin, Qingsong, eds. *China's Rural Industry: Structure, Development and Reform*, New York: Oxford University Press, 1990.

Bull, Clive, "The Existence of Self-Enforcing Implicit Contracts," *Quarterly Journal of Economics*, **102**, 1:147-159, February, 1987.

Cai, Jinyun, "A Study on Legislation on TVEs (Xiangzhen qiye lifa yanjiu)," in Regional Experiment Office of the State Council (ed.), *Gaige sikao lu (A Collection of Studies on*

Reform), pp.195-207.   Beijing: Zhongguo
Zhuoyue Publishing Corp, 1990.

Chen, Kuan, Jefferson, Gary H., Rawski, Thomas G.,
Wang, Hongchang, and Zheng, Yuxin, "New
Estimates of Fixed Investment and Capital Stock
for Chinese State Industry," *China Quarterly*,
114, 2:243-266, June, 1988a.

Chen, Kuan, Jefferson, Gary H., Rawski, Thomas G.,
Wang, Hongchang, and Zheng, Yuxin,
"Productivity Change in Chinese Industry:
1953-1985." *Journal of Comparative Economics*,
12, 4: 570-591, December, 1988b.

Chen, Kang, Jefferson, Gary H., and Singh, Indejit,
"Lessons from China's Economic Reform,"
Journal of Comparative Economics, **16**, 2: 201-
225, June, 1992.

Chen, Xiwen, "The Collective Economy, the Cooperative
Economy and the Stock Cooperative Economy,"
*Chinese Rural Economy (zhongguo nongcun
jingji)*, 11:14-16, November, 1992.

Chen, Yaobang, "tongyi sixiang jiji tiaozheng, cujin
xiangzhen qiye chixu xietiao jiankang fazhan,"
*Chinese Township-Village Enterprise (Zhongguo
xiangzhen qiye)*, 9:1-8, September, 1989.

Chenery, H., et al. (eds.), (1986), *Industrialization and
Growth: A comparative Study*. New York: Oxford
University Press.

China Agricultural Yearbook, 1984, 1986, Beijing: China

Statistical Press. 1984, 1986.

China Daily, July 15, 1992

China Enterprise Management Yearbook (Zhongguo qiye guanli nianjian), 1990, Beijing: Enterprise Management Press, 1990.

Chinese Township-Village Enterprise Yearbook (Zhongguo xiangzhen qiye nianjian), 1990, Beijing: Agricultural Press. 1990.

Christensen, L., D.Cummings, and D.Jorgenson (1980), "Economic Growth, 1947-73: An International Comparison," in J.Kendrick
et al. (eds.), *New Developments in Productivity Measurement and Analysis.* Chicago: University of Chicago Press.

Coase, Ronald H., "The Nature of the Firm," *Economica*, **4**, 4:386-405, November, 1937.

Dasgupta, P., and Ray, D., (1984), "Inequality, Malnutrition and Unemployment: A Critique of Market Mechanism," mimeo.

Deng, Yingtao, "The TVE and Rural Credit," *Rural Economy and Society (nongcun jingji yu shehui)*, No.4, Aprile, 1992.

Demsetz, Harold, "Towards a Theory of Property Rights," *American Economic Review*, **57**, 2:347-359, May, 1967.

Department of Rural Enterprises of Ministry of

Agriculture, China, *A Statistical Survey of Chinese Rural Enterprises 1991 (Chinese edition) (zhongguo xiangzhen qiye tongji zhaiyao 1991)*. Beijing: Reform Press.

Dernberger, Robert M., (1982), "The Chinese Search for the Path of Self-Sustained Growth in the 1980s: An Assessment," in U.S. Congress, Joint Economic Committee, *China Under the Four Modernization*. Vol. 1, pp. 19-76. Washington, D.C.: U.S. Government Printing Office.

Domar, E., (1962), "On Total Productivity and All That," *Journal of Political Economy,* 70:597-608.

Du, Ying, "Joint Stock System Is an Independent Economic Organizational Form (gufen hezuo zhi shi yizhong duli de jingji zuzhi xingtai)," *Chinese Rural Economy (zhongguo nongcun jingji)*, 11:11-13, November, 1992.

Engels, F., (1974), *The Condition of the Working Class in England,* translated from the 1845 edition, England: Panther Press.

Forbes, D., and Linge, G., (1990), "China's Spatial Development: Issues and Prospects," in G.Linge and D.Forbes (eds.), *China's Spatial Economy -- Recent Developments and Reforms*, Hong Kong: Oxford University Press.

Fudenberg, Drew, and Tirole, Jean, *Game Theory,*

Cambridge (Mass): MIT Press, 1992.

Furubotn, Eirik G., and Pejovich, Svetozar, "Introduction: The New Property Rights Literature," in Furubotn, E. and S.Pejovich (eds.), *The Economics of Property Rights*, pp.1-9. Cambridge (Mass.): Ballinger Publishing Company, 1974.

Gelb, Alan, and Svejnar, Jan, "Chinese TVPs in an International Perspective," in Byrd and Lin (eds.), *China's Rural Industry: Structure, Development and Reform*, pp.413-426, New York: Oxford University Press, 1990.

Geng, Dechang (1989), *Quanguo baicun loadongli quingkuang dioacho ziliaoji* (A Nationwide hundred village labor force sample survey), Beijing: Chinese Statistic Press.Harris, J. and Todaro, M. (1970), "Migration unemployment, and development", *AER*, 60:126.

Grossman, Sanford J., and Hart, Oliver D., "The Costs and Benefits of Ownership", *Journal of Political Economy*, **94**, 4:691-719, August 1986.

Harris, J. and Todaro, M. (1970), "Migration, unemployment, and development", *AER*, 60:126.

Hart, Oliver D., and Holmstrom, Bengt, "The Theory

of Contracts", in T. Bewley (ed.), *Advances in Economic Theory, Fifth World Congress*, pp.71-155. Cambridge: Cambridge University Press, 1987.

Hart, Oliver D., and Moore, John, "Property Rights and the Nature of the Firm, *"Journal of Political Economy*, **98**, 6:1119-1158, December, 1990.

He, Kang et al. (eds.), (1980-1986), *Zhongguo Nongye Nianjian [Chinese Agriculture Yearbook], 1980-1986,* Beijing: Agriculture Press.

Ho, X., Liu Y., Liu Y., Wang J (1988), "Xianjieduan Nongcun Shengyu Laodongli Xingwei Tezheng (The behavioral features of rural surplus laborers at the present stage)," *Economic Studies*, No.2.

IESR (Institute of Economic System Reform) (1988), Gaige de Shehui Xinli (The Social Psycology on the Reforms), Chengdu: Sichuan People's Press.Jingji Cankao (Economic Reference), Mar.10, 1987.

Jefferson, Gary H., Rawski, Thomas G., and Zheng, Yuxin, "Growth, Efficiency, and Convergence in China's State and Collective Industry," *Economic Development and Cultural Change*, **40**, 2:239-66, January, 1992.

Jingji cankao (Economic News), March 10, 1987.

Journal of Economic Perspectives, "Symposium on Economic Transition in the Soviet Union and Eastern Europe," **5**, 4, Fall, 1991.

Katz, E. and Stark, O. (1986), "Labor migration and risk aversion in less developed countries," *Journal of Labor Economics*

Kornai, Janos, *The Socialist System*, New York: Princeton University Press and Oxford University Press, 1992.

Kmenta, J., (1967), "On Estimation of CES Production Function." *International Economic Review*, 8: 1880-89.

Kornai, Janos, *The Socialist System*, New York: Princeton University Press and Oxford University Press, 1992.

Kreps, David, "Corporate Culture and Economic Theory", in J.E. Alt and K.A. Shepsle, eds, *Perspectives on Positive Political Economy*. pp.90-143. Cambridge: Cambridge University Press, 1990.

Lau, Kam-Tim, and Brada, Josef C., "Technological Progress and Technical Efficiency in Chinese Industrial Growth: A Frontier Production Function Approach," *China Economic Review*, 2, 1990.Lave, L.B., (1966), *Technological Change: Its Conception and Measurement.*

Englewood Cliffs, N.J.: Prentice-Hall.

Lave, L.B., (1966), *Technological Change: Its Conception and Measurement.* Englewood Cliffs, N.J.: Prentice-Hall.

Leibenstein, H. (1957), "The theory of underemployment in backward economics," *JPE*, 65:91.

Lewis, W. (1954), "Development with unlimited supplies of labor," *Manchester School of Economics and Social Studies*, 20:139.

Lin, Q. (1987), "Shanxi Yuanpingxian Xiangzhen Qiyie Kaocha (An Investigation of TVEs in Yuanping County of Shanxi Province)," in Institute of Economics, CASS (eds.), *Zhongguo Xiangzhen Qiyie de Jingji Fazhan yu Jingji Tizhi (The Economic Development and Economic System of Chinese TVEs)*, Beijing: China's Economics Press.

Lin, Qingsong, "The Reports of the China United Investigation Team on TVE," in the Institute of Economics, CASS (Chinese Academy of Social Sciences) (ed.), *Zhongguo xiangzhen qiye de jingji fazhan yu jingji tizhi (The Economic Development and Economic Institution of China's TVE)*, Beijing: China Economics Press, 1987.

Li Yandong, "Cunban Qiye de Yunxing Jizhi yu Xiangzhen Qiye de Fazhan -- 1986 Nian Nongcun Guding Guanchadian Zhuanti

Fenxi (The Operation Mechanism of VE and the Growth of TVEs -- An Analysis of the Results of 1986 Rural Area Sampling Survey), " Unpublished circulating paper, 1987.

Liu, D., "On Current Disputes of TVE Contracts and their Resolutions," *Nongcun Jingji (Rural Economy)*, No.8, August, 1989.

McMillan, John, and B. Naughton, "How to Reform a Planned Economy: Lessons from China," *Oxford Review of Economic Policy*, 8, Spring, 1992.

Ma Hong, Sun Shangqing, *Zhongguo Jingji Jiegou Wenti Yanjiu (Research on the Problems of Economic Structure in China)*. Beijing: People's Press, 1981.

Ma Hong (ed.), *Xiandai Zhongguo Jingji Shidian (Mini Encyclopedia of Modern Chinese Economy)*. Beijing: CASS Press, 1982. p.213.

Meng Xin, (1990), "The Rural Labor Market," in Byrd and Lin (eds.).

The Ministry of Agriculture, China (ed.), *The PRC(People's Republic of China) Regulations of Rural Collectively-Owned Enterprises (RRCOE) (zhonghua renmin gonghehuo xiangcun jiti suoyou zhi qiye tiaoli)*, Beijing: People's Press. 1990.

Mirrlees, J. (1975), "A Pure Theory of Underdeveloped Economics," in L.Reynolds (ed.), *Agriculture in*

Development Theory, New Haven, CT: Yale University Press.

Naughton, Barry, "What is Distinctive about China's Economic Transition? State Enterprise Reform and Overall System Transformation," mimeo, University of California, San Diego, 1993.

Nee, Victor, "Organizational Dynamics of Market Transition: Hybrid Forms, Property Rights and Mixed Economy in China," *Administrative Science Quarterly*, **37**, 1:1-27, March, 1992.

Oi, Jean, "Fiscal Reform and the Economic Foundations of Local State Corporatism in China," *World Politics*, **45**, 1:99-126, October, 1992.

Perkins, D., and S.Yusuf, (1984), *Rural Development in China*. Baltimore: The Johns Hopkins University Press.

Perkins, D. (1987), "The influence of economic reforms on China's urbanization," a paper prepared for the Conference on Chinese Cities in Asian Context.

Pitt, Mark M., and Putterman, Louis, "Employment and Wages in Township, Village, and other Rural Enterprises," mimeo, Brown University, 1992.Renmin Ribao (haiwai ban) (People's Daily Oversees edition), Feb. 28, 1989.

Ranis, G. and Fei, J. (1961), "A theory of economic development," *AER*, 51:533.

Ravenstein, E. (1889), "The Laws of Migration,"
Journal of the Statistical Society, 52:214-301.

Riskin, C., and J.Sigurdson, (1977), *Rural Industrialization in China*. Cambridge, Mass.: Harvard Council on East Asian Studies.Rosenzweig, M. (1984), "Determinants of Wage Rates and Labor Supply Behavior in the Rural Sector of a Developing Country," in H.P.Binswanger and M.R.Rosenzweig, (eds.), *Contractual Arrangements, Employment and Wages in Rural Labor Markets in Asia*, New Haven, CT: Yale University Press.

Rosenzweig, M. (1988), "Labor markets in low-income countries," in Chenery, H. and Srivinasan, T. (ed.), *Handbook of Development Economics*, Vol 1.

Roumasset, J.A., Boussard, J. and I.Singh (1979), *Risk, Uncertainty and Agricultural Development*, New York: Agricultural Development Council.

Rural Area Investigation Team of the SSB (1987), *Zhongguo Nongcun Zhuhu Jiaji Diaocha (Chinese Rural Household Sample Survey)*, 1987, Beijing: China Statistic Press.

Rural Policy Research Division of the Central Committee Secretariat, Center for Rural Development at the State Council, "A Summary of the All-Nation Rural Socio-economic Sampling Survey," *Zhongguo*

Nongye Nianjian (Chinese Agricultural Yearbook), 1986.

Sen, A. (1966), "Peasants and Dualism with or without surplus labor," *JPE*, 66(5).

Sen, A. (1975), *Employment, Technology and Development*, Oxford University Press.

Sicular, T. (1990) "Ten years of reform: progress and setbacks in agricultural planning and pricing," mimeo.

Song Lina, Du He, (1990),"The Role of Township Governments in RuralIndustrialization," in Byrd and Lin (eds.).

Song Lina, (1990),"Convergence: A Comparison of Township-run Firms and Local State Enterprises," in Byrd and Lin (eds.).

Song, Lina, "Convergence: a comparison of township-run firms and local state enterprises," in Byrd, W. and Q. Lin (eds.), *China's Rural Industry: Structure, Development and Reform*, pp.392-412. New York: Oxford University Press, 1990.

Stark, David, "Path Dependence and Privatization Strategies in East Central Europe," *East European Politics and Societies*, **6**, 1: , Winter, 1992.

Stark, O. (1991), *The Migration of Labor*, Cambridge, MA: Basil Blackwell.

SSB (State Statistical Bureau), (1983-1988),
Zhongguo Tongji Nianjian, 1983-1988
[China Statistical Yearbook, 1983-1988].
Beijing: China Statistics Pub. House.

SSB (State Statistic Bureau) (1989), *Chinese StatisticsYearbook, 1989*, Beijing: Chinese Statistics Press.

Stiglitz, J. (1974), "Alternative theories of wage determination and unemployment in LDCs: the labor turnover model," *QJE*.

Stiglitz, J. (1976), "The efficiency wage hypothesis, surplus labor and the distribution of income in LDCs," *Oxford Economic Papers*, 28.

Svehnar, J. (1990), "Productivity Efficiency an Employment," in Byrd and Lin (eds.).

Svejnar, Jan, "Productive Efficiency and Employment," in Byrd, W. and Q. Lin (eds.), *China's Rural Industry: Structure, Development and Reform*, New York: Oxford University Press, 1990.

Todaro, M. (1969), "A Model of Labor, Migration and Urban Unemployment in Less Developed Countries," *AER*, 59:138-148.

Urban Social and Economic Investigation Team (USEIT) of the State Statistical Bureau (SSB) (1989), *Zhongguo Wujia Tongji Nianjian (China Price Statistical Yearbook)*, Beijing: China Statistic Press.

Wang, Tuoyu, (1990), "Regional Imbalance," in Byrd

and Lin (eds.).

Williamson, Oliver, *The Economic Institutions of Capitalism*, New York: Free Press, 1985.

Wong, C., (1989), "Maoism and Development: A Reconsideration of Local Self-reliance in Financing Rural Industrialization," in W.Joseph, C.Wong, and D.Zweig (eds.) *New Perspectives on the Cultural Revolution.* Cambridge, Mass.: Harvard University Press.

Wong, C., (1988), "Interpreting Rural Industrial Growth in the Post-Mao Period," *Modern China*, 14(1).

Woo, Wing-Tye, Hai, Wen, Jin, Y., and Fan, Gang, "How Successful Has Enterprise Reform Been?" mimeo, University of California, Davis, 1993.

World Bank, (1985), *China Long-term Development Issues and Options.* Baltimore: Johns Hopkins University Press.

Wu Quhui, Wang Hansheng, and Xu Xinxin, (1990), "Noneconomic Factors Determining Workers' Income," in Byrd and Lin (eds.).

Wu, Quhui, Wang, Hansheng, and Xu, Xinxin, "Noneconomic Factors Determining Workers' Income," in Byrd, W. and Q. Lin (eds.), *China's Rural Industry: Structure, Development and Reform*, pp.323-338. New York: Oxford University Press, 1990.

Development and Reform, pp.323-338. New York: Oxford University Press, 1990.

Xu, Chenggang, "Productivity and Behavior of Chinese Rural Industrial Enterprises," Chapter 1 of this volume, 1994.

Zhoucun Rural Reform Experimental Regional Office (ZZERO), *Zhoucun Xianxiang*, mimeo, Zhoucun District (Shandong Province): Zhoucun Rural Reform Experimental Regional Office, 1992.

INDEX

Agriculture (7), (15), (18), (19), (41), (53), (72), (75), (99), (100-102), (107), (108), (110), (111), (113), (114), (119), (124-126)

American Rural Small-scale Industry Delegation (9)

Autonomy (10), (15), (20), (28), (74), (76)

Bankrupt (78)

Behavior of TVEs (vii), (4), (11), (12), (21), (24), (33), (50)

Bergson, A. (44)

Brigades (12), (20)

Bureaucratic control (11), (18)

Bureaucratic hierarchy (13)

Capitalism (61), (67), (86-88)

CBE (12), (14)

Central government (10), (14), (15), (19), (20), (28), (29)

CES function (25), (26), (30)

Chenery, H. (44)

Chinese economy (x), (3), (8), (9), (14-17), (101), (107), (124)

Coastal region (26), (27), (32), (47)

Cobb-Douglas function (25-27)

Collectively-owned enterprises (4), (9), (14), (16), (18), (19), (22), (28), (29), (33), (69), (73), (74), (75), (76)

Communes (12), (20)

Conflicts (5), (64), (79), (82), (84)

Constant elasticity of substitution (25)

For Product Safety Concerns and Information please contact our EU
representative GPSR@taylorandfrancis.com Taylor & Francis Verlag GmbH,
Kaufingerstraße 24, 80331 München, Germany

Printed and bound by CPI Group (UK) Ltd, Croydon, CR0 4YY
08/05/2025
01864369-0004